BY KAREEM KENNEDY

Aunt Alice vs. Bob Marley

My Education in New Orleans

Neighborhood Story Project

P.O. Box 19742

New Orleans, LA 70179

www.neighborhoodstoryproject.org

Editor: Rachel Breunlin

Publisher: Abram Himelstein

Graphic Designer: Gareth Breunlin

The printing of this book made possible by
a generous grant from the Lupin Foundation.

THE

LUPIN

FOUNDATION

ISBN-13: 978-1-60801-013-4

Library of Congress Control Number: 2009940210

http://unopress.org

Dedication

To my family, the memory of Martin Luther King, Malcolm X, Marcus Garvey, and Bob Marley and kids growing up in the struggle—keep on moving.

Acknowledgments

I want to thank all of the people who have been supportive of me and the book.

To Rachel, Abram, Lea and Lindsey of the Neighborhood Story Project for your time and dedication to making this book a reality, and for being by my side through battles.

To Daron, Kenneth, Susan, and Pernell: For being so dedicated to the writing. It's been a long time coming and we are here.

To my book committee: April, Mario, G.K., and Branden. Thank you.

To Martin Luther King, Jr., Marcus Garvey, Bob Marley, Malcom X—brothers who taught me about Blackness and pride.

To my Aunt Alice—you tried when you could have given up.

To John Washington—thanks for being a real man and showing me how to take care of business.

To Marlene, Steven, Malika, Douglas, April, Ashley, Kaiema, Hakim, and Hason—I wish success and happiness to you all and remember, "Blood is thicker than water."

To Menard Nelson, Langston Hughes, Gregory Junior High, John F. Kennedy, Alief Hastings, John McDonogh, Delgado Community College—passing through your doors, I took something with me from each of you.

To Brother Rob for teaching me about economics, politics and Black history, which enhanced my thinking.

To Mr. Reilhmann for introducing me to "A Dream Deferred" and "A Negro Speaks."

To Sarah Fisher, Rachel Nicolosi, Hazel Parker, and my fellow Literacy Americorps members.

To the medical staff over on the eighth floor of University—you guys are the best.

To Ms. Rauser's 2009 Eighth Grade Capdau students. Y'all reminded me so much of myself and your writing truly inspired my own.

To Barack Obama for taking leadership and promoting change.

To God for putting strength in my body and for giving me time.

To New Orleans—no place like home.

To the New Orleans Saints for giving me something to get emotional about—Who Dat?!

To Larry, Ray, Kadeem, Ken, Bell, Alberta, Eminem, Tre'mall, Joe, Kenneth, Jonathan, George, Doug, Bernie Mac, Tupac, Christopher, Black, Mr. Andy, Otis, Luther, Diamond, and Jerome.

To Miriam for being with me through the good, bad, and ugly, and showering me with unconditional positive regard—til we meet again.

To Mario, Jason, Malad, Kendall, Rody, Ronald, Greg, B-Lo, India—strong brothers and sisters who listened with open ears about my journeys and frustrations.

Table of Contents

THE ORIGINAL
MARBLE COVER-48 SHEETS

NAME _Reen_

WIDE RULED
ROARING SPRING, PA 16673

The Message

"Young, Black & Positive"

A young scholar making a path to better himself, through writing books, working, and attending school. My books consist of real-life stories about living in the 7 ward. I want to tell the stories that haven't been told. Through my eyes you'll get a taste of New Orleans it's moments of triumph and also despair.

Introductions

Journal Entry

Mary Jane is the ultimate pain and stress reliever it wor better tylanol and aspirin. It takes you to a peace state of mind and gives eagle vision. Mary Jane opens up your spiritual side of your mind it makes you forget about the harshness of reality and the cruelty of man. Natural herb is the best. Police officers think that smokers are dumb and weed heads but they don't know w be in a different zone we be in a chill mode se like. If Mary Jane was legal the courts wouldn't b to crowded with smokers who get caught for simple po estion. I love a smoking session when it's me and m lil dogs reminishing about them good old days, lust fr and the future. You tend to see things in a different light your mind racing with wild thoughts. I like to consume a blunt when I study or when I'm doing research. The aroma of that stick of herbs smells so potent in the air.

"Get up, Stand Up"

People tell me, "You're a young man with an old soul." But my youngness, in the eyes of some people, supersedes my old soul. Several times, my outer appearance as a Black man with dreadlocks has been stereotyped as gangsta, and as a result, my place in the world has been antagonized.

At an early age, my old soul began experimenting with marijuana, looking for a way to cope with my frustrations and pain. It became a part of my lifestyle, and I sought out the Jamaican subculture of Rastafarianism because Rastas weren't rich but believed in humbleness and the praising of Blacks. Bob Marley's "Get Up, Stand Up" became my theme. My curly locks gave me the feeling of pride greater than the mightiest beast in the jungle.

During my last year of high school, I also made the decision to apply for a spot in the Neighborhood Story Project. I had always been fascinated by literature. Growing up, I kept my nose in novels, newspapers, and textbooks because I liked getting to know other people's lives. Walking in the shoes of characters through places, events, and history eased my mind. I realized the influence writing had on an individual's growth and development.

I wasn't sure what I was getting into, but I knew that other writers in the NSP had left a lasting impression on the city. As I began to write, I thought to myself, "Hey, somebody going through similar struggles can use this." I began with random thoughts and positive messages. At the same time, I was often heckled by cops for possession of weed, or just because they thought I was up to no good. Getting arrested brought back all my anxieties as I passed through the most violent, corrupted place in the city—Orleans Parish Prison. I knew I didn't want to end up behind bars.

Self-portrait, by Kareem Kennedy.

☒ INCIDENT REPORT	ITEM NUMBER
☐ SUPPLEMENTAL REPORT 1 OF 81	D-29931-08

EVENT

SIGNAL	INCIDENT	DATE/TIME OCCURRED	DIST/ZONE/SUB	STATUS	BULLETIN REQUIRED
966	Drug Law Violation	04.23.2008 / 3:55 p.m.	1/J/04	☐ OPEN ☒ CLEARED BY ARREST ☐ CLEARED BY EXCEPT. ☐ WARRANT ISSUED ☐ UNFOUNDED	☐ YES ☒ NO
LOCATION OF OCCURANCE		DATE/TIME OF REPORT	LIGHTING		
1000 block of North Dorgenois Street		04.23.2008 / 3:55 p.m.	G		

VICTIM/REPORTING PERSON

☒ VICTIM ☐ WITNESS ☐ REPORTING PERSON ☐ INTERVIEW		DATE OF BIRTH OR AGE	RACE	SEX	VICTIM TYPE	VICTIM #
State of Louisiana		X	X	X	G	01
HOME ADDRESS	ZIP CODE	HOME PHONE	SOCIAL SECURITY NUMBER	SOBRIETY	INJURY	TREATED
X	X	X	X	X	X	X
BUSINESS ADDRESS	ZIP CODE	BUSINESS PHONE	DRIVERS LICENSE NUMBER	OCCUPATION		
X	X	X	X	X		

☐ VICTIM ☐ WITNESS ☐ REPORTING PERSON ☐ INTERVIEW		DATE OF BIRTH OR AGE	RACE	SEX	VICTIM TYPE	VICTIM #
X		X	X	X	X	X
HOME ADDRESS	ZIP CODE	HOME PHONE	SOCIAL SECURITY NUMBER	SOBRIETY	INJURY	TREATED
X	X	X	X	X	X	X
BUSINESS ADDRESS	ZIP CODE	BUSINESS PHONE	DRIVERS LICENSE NUMBER	OCCUPATION		
X	X	X	X	X		

OFFENDER NO. 1

☒ ARRESTED ☐ WANTED ☐ MISSING ☐ RUNAWAY		DATE OF BIRTH OR AGE	RACE	SEX	HEIGHT	WEIGHT
Kennedy, Kareem		10/31/89	B	M	5'7"	165 lbs.
HOME ADDRESS	ZIP CODE	DATE/TIME OF ARREST	ARREST CREDIT	SOBRIETY	INJURY	TREATED
3014 Bruxelles Street	70122	04.23.2008 / 3:55 p.m.	70	U	N	N/A
ARREST LOCATION		SOCIAL SECURITY NUMBER	DRIVERS LICENSE NUMBER	DIST/ZONE/SUB	RIGHTS WAIVED FORM #	
1000 block of North Dorgenois Street			NONE	1/J/04	VERBAL	
ALIAS/NICKNAME		MAGISTRATE DATE/TIME		TRANSPORTED BY		UNIT
NONE		TO BE SET		Jones		4862

ARREST&EE ARMED AT TIME OF ARREST			ARREST TYPE		RESIDENT STATUS	JUVENILE DISPOSITION
☒ UNARMED ☐ HANDGUN	☐ SHOTGUN ☐ RIFLE	☐ KNIFE ☐ OTHER WEAPON	☐ AUTOMATIC ☐ SEMI-AUTOMATIC	☒ ON VIEW ☐ EXISTING WARRANT ☐ SUMMONS	☒ ORLEANS RESIDENT ☐ NON-RESIDENT	☐ RELEASED TO PARENT ☐ HELD FOR COURT

CHARGES	VICTIM #	RELATIONSHIP
R.S. 40:966 Relative to Possession of a Schedule I Controlled Dangerous Substance, to wit;	01	S
Marijuana.		

DESCRIPTION

01-BUILD	02-ODDITIES	03-SCARS	04-TATTOOS	05-APPAREL	06-SPEECH
☐ 01 SMALL/PETITE ☒ 02 THIN ☐ 03 MEDIUM ☐ 04 MUSCULAR ☐ 05 HEAVY/STOCKY ☐ 06 FLABBY ☐ 07 STOOPED SHOULDERS ☐ 08 NARROW SHOULDERS ☐ 09 BROAD SHOULDERS ☐ 10 DWARF/MIDGET	☐ 01 LIMP ☐ 02 CRIPPLED ARM ☐ 03 MISSING ARM ☐ 04 MISSING FINGER ☐ 05 MISSING HAND ☐ 06 MISSING FOOT ☐ 07 MISSING LEG ☐ 08 ABNORMAL GENITALS ☐ 09 BODY ODOR ☐ 10 LEFT HANDED	☐ 01 CHEEK, LEFT ☐ 02 CHEEK, RIGHT ☐ 03 CHIN ☐ 04 EAR, LEFT ☐ 05 EAR, RIGHT ☐ 06 EYEBROW, LEFT ☐ 07 EYEBROW, RIGHT ☐ 08 LIP UPPER ☐ 09 NOSE ☐ 10 NECK ☐ 11 ARM, LEFT ☐ 12 ARM, RIGHT ☐ 13 HAND, LEFT ☐ 14 HAND, RIGHT ☐ 15 WRIST, LEFT ☐ 16 WRIST, RIGHT ☐ 17 CHEST ☐ 18 BACK ☐ 19 LEG, LEFT ☐ 20 LEG, RIGHT	☐ 01 ARM, LEFT ☐ 02 ARM, RIGHT ☐ 03 HAND, LEFT ☐ 04 HAND, RIGHT ☐ 05 LEG, LEFT ☐ 06 LEG, RIGHT ☐ 07 CHEST ☐ 08 NECK ☐ 09 BACK ☐ 10 FACE	☐ 01 CLOTH OVER FACE ☐ 02 STOCKING OVER FACE ☐ 03 MASK ☐ 04 EARRINGS ☐ 05 SUNGLASSES ☐ 06 RINGS ☐ 07 GLOVES ☐ 08 CAP/HAT ☒ 09 MAN-FEMALE ATTIRE ☒ 10 TENNIS SHOES	☐ 01 SOFT/POLITE ☐ 02 RASPY/DEEP ☐ 03 RAPID ☐ 04 SLOW ☐ 05 LOUD ☐ 06 MUMBLE ☐ 07 STUTTERS/LISP ☐ 08 VULGAR ☐ 09 APOLOGETIC ☐ 10 EFFEMINATE

07-ACCENT	08-FACIAL ODDITIES	09-EYES	10-NOSE	11-TEETH	12-HAIR COLOR	13-HAIR STYLE	14-FACIAL HAIR	15-COMPLEXION
☐ 01 AFRO/AMERICAN ☐ 02 SPANISH ☐ 03 ORIENTAL ☐ 04 FRENCH ☐ 05 ENGLISH ☐ 06 JAMAICAN ☐ 07 OTHER	☐ 01 BIRTHMARKS ☐ 02 BLOTCHES ☐ 03 FRECKLES ☐ 04 MOLE/WARTS ☐ 05 PIMPLE/POCKS ☐ 06 WRINKLES ☐ 07 HIGH CHEEKS ☐ 08 THICK LIPS ☐ 09 DEFORMED EAR ☐ 10 MISSING EAR	☐ 01 BLUE ☒ 02 BROWN ☐ 03 GREY ☐ 04 GREEN ☐ 05 BLOODSHOT ☐ 06 BULGING ☐ 07 CROSSED ☐ 08 MISSING/GLASS ☐ 09 SQUINTS/BLINKS ☐ 10 SLANTED/ORIENTAL	☐ 01 LARGE ☐ 02 SMALL ☐ 03 LONG ☐ 04 THIN ☐ 05 PUG ☐ 06 POINTED ☐ 07 BROAD ☐ 08 FLAT ☐ 09 HOOKED ☐ 10 RED	☐ 01 IRREGULAR ☐ 02 DECAYED ☐ 03 PROTRUDING ☐ 04 CAPS ☐ 05 MISSING ☐ 06 CHIPPED ☐ 07 GOLD ☐ 08 DESIGN ☐ 09 DIAMOND ☐ 10 BRACES	☐ 01 BLONDE ☐ 02 RED ☒ 03 BROWN ☐ 04 BLACK ☐ 05 GREY/SILVER ☐ 06 SALT/PEPPER ☐ 07 MULTI-COLOR ☐ 08 PLAT. BLONDE ☐ 09 STREAKED ☐ 10 GREY PATCHES	☐ 01 AFRO ☐ 02 BRAIDED ☐ 03 CURLY ☐ 04 STRAIGHT ☐ 05 CREWCUT ☐ 06 BALD ☐ 07 SHORT ☒ 08 MEDIUM ☐ 09 LONG ☐ 10 FADE/DESIGN	☐ 01 SIDEBURNS ☐ 02 MUTTON CHOPS ☐ 03 BEARD ☐ 04 GOATEE ☐ 05 MUSTACHE ☐ 06 FU-MANCHU ☐ 07 HAIR UND. LIP ☐ 08 UNSHAVEN ☐ 09 BUSHY EYEBROWS ☐ 10 CLEAN SHAVEN	☐ 01 ALBINO ☐ 02 FAIR ☐ 03 RUDDY ☐ 04 OLIVE ☐ 05 LIGHT ☐ 06 BROWN ☒ 07 DARK

ADDITIONAL DESCRIPTION

Black 'dickie" shirt, Black "dickie" pants.

CODES

RACE	VICTIM TYPE	SOBRIETY	INJURY	TREATED	VICTIM RELATIONSHIP TO OFFENDER (VICTIM WAS:)		
W-WHITE B-BLACK I-AMERIND A-ASIAN U-UNKNOWN	B-BUSINESS F-FINACIAL INST. G-GOVERNMENT L-LAW OFFICER R-RELIGIOUS ORG.	S-SOCIETY C-ORLEANS RESIDENT M-METRO RESIDENT N-NON RESIDENT U-UNKNOWN	S-SOBER A-ALCOHOL D-DRUGS U-UNKNOWN	B-BROKEN BONES H-INTERNAL INJURY L-LACERATIONS M-MINOR O-OTHER MAJOR N-NO INJURY	R-REFUSED T-TREATED H-HOSPITALIZED	A-SPOUSE B-COMMON LAW C-PARENT D-OFFSPRING E-SIBLING F-GRANDPARENT	G-GRANDCHILD H-OTHER FAMILY I-ACQUAINTANCE J-NEIGHBOR K-BEING BABYSAT L-BOY/GIRL FRIEND	M-EX SPOUSE N-EMPLOYEE O-EMPLOYER P-HOMOSEXUAL S-STRANGER U-UNKNOWN

ADM

DETECTIVE	CRIME LAB	OTHER	REPORTING CAR #
Ray Jones Badge #975	N/A	N/A	4874
REPORTING OFFICER	BADGE	REPORTING OFFICER	BADGE	SUPERVISOR	BADGE
P/O IV Leonard Davis	2345	P/O IV D. Burmaster	961	NICOLE BARBE	439

6

Previous page and above: Kareem's citation from the New Orleans Police Department in April 2008.

After sleeping a couple of nights behind bars, I wrote:

I thought Mary Jane was harmless. Huh. Got me seven whole days of headache and mental breaking. From the guards ignoring the hell out of you to the ignorance and arrogance of the other inmates, I hate it all. But there is something to learn: It is God's will. I know he will give me light when there is darkness. I know he'll show me the path of righteousness. He put me through trials to make me stronger and wiser. He chose to put me there so I can gather my thoughts and refocus on my goal of bettering society by using knowledge and understanding.

I wish I could speak a piece of my mind to the world. I would let the world know to stop being fools—to start living. I would tell them: "Erase hate and bad attitudes, *and start adding peace and freewill." I wish I could open the hearts of the young and poor to encourage them to start making positive changes in their lives. I would tell them, "Just because you're not rich, it doesn't mean anything. Wealth just means you earned more paper, not necessarily respect." I would tell them to honor and respect people as human beings and not rely on religion, outward appearance, or affiliation to determine that.*

My message sounded good in my journal, but it was too idealistic. I needed to make some pragmatic changes. I knew I was getting profiled for my dreads after the cops told me, "You need to cut that shit off." My boss at a Seventh Ward carwash agreed: "You look like everybody else around here, you should get a fresh cut." I decided to cut my hair.

The St. Bernard Housing Development, by Kareem Kennedy.

My Hood

My writing coaches, Abram and Rachel, told me my writing was "too abstract," which meant I didn't give enough detail, so I began to dig up tales from the hood. Growing up in the Seventh Ward and the St. Bernard Public Housing Development of New Orleans—it's like you're being a sponge, soaking up all the good and bad things.

Growing up, I knew that I was poor and learned to be tough in the streets. Occasionally, I got in fights because kids made fun of my previous-year school uniforms and old Nikes. But the project used to be so alive, like a drummer beating his drum. I reminisced hanging on the porch with my homies, ribbing, talking about chicks and smoking. Writing after Hurricane Katrina made me appreciate everything about my hood. With the older folks, respect and team always came first. I remember when my Aunt Rose used to send me to the store with a list and tell me to make sure to bring back the receipt. As I was walking, if I noticed Papa Henry struggling, bringing out the trash, I would lend him a hand. I wrote about the little pleasures like coming home from school with my aces and walking up the courtway to snatch a couple of frozen cups from Ms. Urline who lived on the first floor. Tutti Fruity was my favorite because she would put real fruit in it.

These stories came to me easily, but my family stories were harder to write. I was a juvenile; emotionally scarred from the absence of mother and father. My aunt pushed me to succeed in school and made sure I had a roof over my head, but I had been pretty much on my own since ninth grade. Aside from the essence of Aunt Alice lingering in my mind, the streets became the front line of my learning. I knew the lines of the poet Langston Hughes just as well as I knew how to play hookie.

One day, I finally wrote about my family and kept it real. Many people think because of my calm and quiet demeanor that things going on around me don't affect me. Now, my deepest thoughts started to come together in writing.

Kareem on Bruxelles, by Lindsey Darnell.

~~First~~ Family Life

I come from a large group of siblings
(9) of us all together. Names/Steven, Douglas, Malika,
Ashely, April, Kiena, Hason, and Hakim. ~~some of us~~ Even
though we are brothers and sisters we ~~were~~ never
lived together. ~~The reason being is that my mother~~
Marlene which is my mother gave ~~birth~~ life to us.
My dad's name is Douglass. The reason why we
didn't @ grow-up together is because of my mother's
drug addiction and my father in and out of jail,
which forced us to live in separation. Since our
parents couldn't raise us I other kind hearts stepped
in. When I was younger my aunt Alice came
by to see me in the projects, she saw that I
was not being property taken care of so she
took me with her to nurture me and she
did so @ from a baby until about age 14-15.
She also tried to do for my sisters and brothers
Steven, Douglass ~~and Malika~~ Malika and ~~my~~ Percy my cousin.
Alice maintained for a while but was overwhelmed

Ashley and April
Kennedy 178 6 1 2 1 9

My Family

I come from a large group of siblings, nine of us all together. Names: Steven, Douglas, Malika, Ashley, April, Kierra, Hason, and Hakim. Even though we are brothers and sisters, we never lived together. Marlene, who is my mother, gave life to us. My dad's name is Douglas. The reason why we didn't grow up together is because of my mother's drug addiction and my father in and out of jail, which forced us to live in separation. Since our parents couldn't raise us, other kind hearts stepped in. When I was younger, my aunt Alice came by the projects. She saw I wasn't being properly taken care of, so she took me with her to nurture me. She did so from a baby until age 14. She also tried to do for my sisters and brothers Steven, Douglas, and Malika. Plus my cousin Percy and her own kids.

Growing up, a sensation of emptiness swelled in me when I was asked to complete a document that required me to fill in my mother's and father's names. I didn't know how to explain that my mother was an addict and I had never met my father.

My mother is a short, slender, and beautiful woman.

I don't recall any significant memories of me and her until about the age of seven. During the summer time, my Aunt Alice would drop me off at my grandmother's apartment in the St. Bernard because she had to work a day job. My grandmother usually prepared me breakfast—often oatmeal, which I hated, or donuts from Mrs. Silvia's Store. After I ate, she would tell me to go play in the courtyard. My mother would come through the cut and say, "Hey KoKo." I knew it was my mother because her voice and face had been programmed in my head. She would give me a tight hug, kiss me on my forehead, and say "Aunt Alice being mean to you?"

I would say, "Yes."

"Don't worry, Mama going to get us a house." Then she'd yell to my grandmother that she was taking me with her. We would walk to where she lived in a third floor apartment with her best friend's family.

In the project, practically everyone was family and many were going through the same struggles. The household was family-full and played the role of sweet shop in the bricks. I remember Tamara,

Previous page: Kareem's notebook. *Above:* Marlene's children Steven, Ashley and April, Douglas, Malika, Kareem and Kaiema, Hakim and Hason.

Doorway into an apartment in the St. Bernard, by Kareem Kennedy.

Twanda, "Fat Cat," Romalace "Rody," Jeffrey, my mom's best friend (whose name also was Marlene), and Ms. Mel, her mother, vividly. My mom would camp out in the kitchen/sweetshop with Ms. Mel smoking cigarettes and talking loud.

When I first started visiting my "god family," it felt like I was a mouse placed in a lion's den. When I'd venture into the teenagers' room, everyone seemed to do whatever they wanted—posters of naked girls hung on the door, dozens of Nikes were scattered on the floor, and three beds were crammed into the room.

My mom would leave with her friend and tell me to, "Be good. I'll be right back." Ms. Mel would give me a frozen cup and tell me to go play in the driveway or the courtyard. I used to hook up with the kids my age and play kool-can or pitch-up tackle. Everyone knew that I was Marlene's son. They would ask, "Where's your twin?" confusing me with Hakim and Hason, my younger twin brothers. Other people who knew my dad would say, "You his son, huh? You look just like him."

By the time I made it back upstairs, my mom would be in the kitchen with bags full of underwear, socks, and undershirts. She gave them to me and said, "Mama got you this." She also brought little Hot Wheels cars and action figures. Then she would walk me back to my grandmother's house and tell me, "I love you, KoKo" and kiss me on the forehead goodbye. My grandmother would give me money to get food from Spider's, where I'd buy a white to-go box filled with drumettes and wings covered with the spiciest hot sauce in the city. My aunt would pick me up about five each evening. She'd chat it up with my grandmother and then we would go home.

Rage and anger boiled inside of me through my childhood years and still have their side effects. I picked and stumbled into countless fights because of that conflict with myself. When I got into fights with kids from the neighborhood and their parents got involved I would verbally chew them out. My aunt constantly battled me out of situations that would've sent me to a juvenile facility or foster home. She always defended me with the fact that I was a child of a broken home.

Steven Kennedy, by Kareem Kennedy.

Interview with My Brother, Steven Kennedy

After Katrina, I was living with my brother Steven for the first time since I was small. Our FEMA trailer had one small restroom, two bunk beds, one sofa bed, which had a small storage space underneath, one small stove, and air filled with sickness (formaldehyde). Normal rain made the trailers feel like you were in the middle of a monsoon, swaying and rocking as thunderstorms passed. It was like we were on an extended camping trip—my brother, uncle, and me. In the morning it felt like the tin can had a clogged artery because getting around was difficult with three grown men trying to maneuver through a narrow space. At night, I would shower like an elephant with its trunk—hose and soap in hand. The best thing about the tin can came on Sunday when the Saints played—win or lose. If you passed by during a game, you'd hear me whooping and hollering when they scored and cussing when they fumbled or threw an interception.

My brother is always overloading me with knowledge. Whether it is about surviving the streets or talking about urban development, he keeps me informed. When I was younger I watched his involvement with the drug game. He always had a nice car with a beautiful girl in it. He slept at Aunt Alice's sometimes and would put the money he made in his shoe. In my curiosity, I stumbled upon a roll of money which inspired awe. I had never seen two-dollar bills before, so I decided to keep six of them. He realized he was short, and told me not to steal from him—all I had to do was ask.

As I began working on this book, I had something else to ask of him. I wanted to do an interview with him about our family. He said he would and I got the chance to listen to him talk about his struggles to raise himself and become a man, not a statistic.

13

Left: Steven in the St. Bernard. *Right:* Steven at school with Aunt Alice. Photographs courtesy of Steven Kennedy.

Kareem: What's good, Steve?

Steven: Nothing much. Same old, same old.

Kareem: Where did you grow up?

Steven: I grew up in the St. Bernard Housing Development.

Kareem: How are you connected with St. Bernard?

Steven: Now that it has been torn down, I'm just connected by my past when I talk to people that I grew up with, my family members.

Kareem: Could you describe the neighborhood?

Steven: Oh man. Growing up in the projects was a double-edged sword. By my mother being on drugs and my father not there, I learned a lot of negative stuff, but I also learned a lot of different personalities. It was a harsh environment, let's put it that way.

Kareem: When did you start living with Aunt Alice?

Steven: I started living with her around 1990. My mother went to prison, so I was around 12.

Kareem: Could you explain a little bit more about why you lived with her?

Steven: Growing up in a dysfunctional family, I had to go with whoever would accept me and my brothers and my sisters.

Kareem: What was it like growing up with no parents to look after you?

Steven: Growing up with no parents created a lot of anger in me, and a sense of distrust. It was hard to love. I developed a sense of hopelessness at times. Even if they were in the project, you'd still see people with their mama or daddy, and you'd be like, "Damn." It created an envy, like, "Why aren't my parents there?"

Kareem: How did you cope with that?

Steven: Got into the streets. Began doing typical stuff that was around me that I felt was righteous—selling drugs and doing other little crimes.

Kareem: Can you tell me your relationship with your mom and dad?

Steven: I'll start with my father. I can't say it's a relationship. I love him, but I feel like, "Come on, dude. You made this choice. You made a child and then you just up and leave?" He doesn't have to be there financially. Just be there to give me some guidance. I not only feel the pain for me, I feel it for my other brothers and sisters, even though we don't share both of the same parents.

I love my mother. She gave me birth and she was around more than he was. I guess I give her more leeway because she's a female and she let herself succumb to drugs. I love her, but it's from a distance now.

Kareem: Can you tell me about a time when you felt close with Ma?

Steven: When both of us were in prison, that's probably the closest I ever felt to her because we were corresponding. It was like, "Okay, now we communicating." She was hitting me with spirituality scripts and talking about life issues. She was telling me she was sorry for not being there. She was off of drugs and I guess her mind and her body were at peace.

Kareem: What was it like being the oldest of nine children?

Steven: Shit, it was difficult. I'd try to be the father to my brothers and sisters, which I try to still do. But it's hard when you're doing wrong. It's like, "Do as I say but not as I do." I was a contradiction.

Kareem: What was it like growing up with Aunt Alice in a house full of people?

Steven: I developed a lot of animosity towards her

because she always used to fuss. But when I got older, I was loving her and thought, "Okay, that's why she wanted us to get an education, to be able to live in a nice environment." She stayed on Bruxelles—that's in Gentilly, off of Paris Avenue. It was a working-class neighborhood. There wasn't a lot of hanging, or open drug dealing.

Kareem: What do you remember most growing up with Aunt Alice?

Steven: When I was younger, she would drive us through all these nice neighborhoods to inspire us. She was a housekeeper for people called the Zuparto's, a wealthy family in New Orleans, and she took us by their house on Lake Shore Drive and another subdivision that's across the street from Bayou St. John. She'd be like, "You see these nice homes? You gotta get yourself educated so you can live like this because nobody in our family is educated." We were coming from the projects and neighborhoods where we saw trash and beer bottles. We were like, "Damn. Yeah, this nice." She'd do it on the weekends or—

Kareem: On errands, too. What was our relationship growing up?

Steven: Well, I was living with my aunt and you were living with my mother and her friend who were on drugs. And then when I wound up leaving and going to Boys Town, you wound up moving by my aunt. It wasn't like we were always communicating.

Kareem: How old were you when you went to Boys Town?

Steven: It was in 1994. I had to be 14 years old.

Kareem: Why did you go to Boys Town?

Steven: I got kicked out of John McDonogh the first day of school. They performed a sweep and I was gambling so I got kicked out. The probation officer wound up talking to my aunt and referred her to Father Bob Allanch. He was a teacher at Jesuit and had a little program, Boys Hope.

I ended up moving to Boys Town in Nebraska, a group home that put dysfunctional youth in a family environment. It was the best place I could have been in my life. Being a delinquent youth, not having a mother or father, and taking a wrong path, it's the only way I would ever finish school and break the cycle that I was living.

We had people called "FTs," family teachers. It was a male and a female that had to be married. They had their little kids and we lived in nice homes—probably $300,000.00 homes. That's where I first learned about chores and learned how to cook. Each week, we were assigned to a chore. Each day, we had to cook a meal. I had a roommate and I had four different families because each one of them would leave for their own reasons.

Kareem: Did you feel like you was getting tossed around at that point from family to family?

Steven: I was kind of happy because sometimes I'd be thinking, "Damn, they're getting on my nerves." We had this point system. If you got a write-up in school, you lost a certain amount of points and a certain amount of privileges. You'd probably have to clean up or cut the lawn. I had a problem with authority and still kind of have a problem with authority.

Kareem: Did Boys Town give you a new perspective on life?

Steven: Oh, man. That's where I met one of my best friends to this day—a guy named Harry Moore from Chicago. That's my first time interacting with white people and Hispanics. It was a real diverse environment. By living in the projects, you just have a projects perspective. You don't have a perspective of the world and other cultures. I was always taught, "Don't trust white people." But that wasn't true. It broadened my horizon.

New Orleans is an open city. You just have that assurance where you're walking up the street and you can speak to somebody and be like, "What's up man," and people will speak back. But when you're living out of town, you speak and they just look at you. And what else? It snowed. Snow was one thing I never saw before. And cornfields. Omaha was not really an urban environment to me.

Kareem: Why did you decide to come back to New Orleans?

Steven: I came back to New Orleans in May 1997 for the summer break before I went to college.

Kareem: Do you think it was a smart move?

Steven: I think it was the worst move I could have made in my life, man, to be honest. When I came back for the little summertime, I got back into my street mentality. Went to selling drugs again just from being around my friends and family members who were selling. I'm like, "Shit, I might as well make some money." That's all it basically was—instant gratification.

Kareem: How has incarceration affected you?

Steven: God, it made me a convicted felon. It makes people who don't even know you be judgmental. I think I was going on 21, and I had federal and state charges. I was convicted in federal court and also state court. I did time in Beaumont, Texas and in Yazoo City, Mississippi in federal facilities, and I also did time in DeQuincy, Louisiana at a state facility.

Kareem: If you could do it all over again, would you?

Steven: Meaning the street life?

Kareem: Yeah.

Steven: Oh man, if I could change that, it would probably be the best thing I could ever do in my life. It's the only thing I would want to change. When you're in prison, you have a lot of time to think and you feel separated from everybody. Whatever time frame you were on with other people, it stops when you go to prison. The only people you exist to are inside those prison walls. On the outside, you're not existing at all.

Kareem: What was it like when you were finally released?

Steven: It was like falling in love with a female for the first time. It was like, "Damn, I'm free." You don't appreciate your freedom and the simple things until it's taken away from you. Every little thing was exciting to me and it made me look at people differently and cherish relationships more.

Kareem: What does your tattoo represent?

Steven: My hood, where I grew up, violence. It's a joker with a gun with some project buildings and my initials. I was in Yazoo when I got it done. When you're in jail, people are creative. I met some of the greatest thinkers in there.

Kareem: What motivated you to change your past life and live the one you have now?

Steven: Shit, prison. Like I said, going to the library, laying in the cell and reading on different people like Warren Buffet making power moves. I was like, "Damn, I've gotta get my piece of the pie." I was gaining this knowledge and understanding about life and really understanding about money.

Kareem: What books did you read while you were incarcerated that you remember?

Steven: God, I read *The Prophet* by Khalil Gibran. I read *As a Man Thinketh* by James Allen. I read *Mis-Education of the Negro* by Dr. Carter G. Woodson. I read *Soul on Ice* by Eldridge Cleaver. I wrote a poem about that, too. I read *The Souls of Black Folk*. I read *Invisible Man* by Ralph Ellison. I read Sister Souljah's *The Coldest Winter Ever*. I read everything I could get my hand on. It made me feel good. It expanded my vocabulary. Reading books about Sigmund Freud and Nietzsche gave me insight about how other people think and I was like, "Okay, now I can kind of relate." I wanted to learn a broad perspective about life.

Kareem: Did you get discriminated when you grew up in the hood?

Steven: I don't think you can really have racial dis-crimination within the project where you're all in the same predicament. But as far as white America, and police officers, yeah.

Kareem: How has the death and incarceration of close friends affected you?

Steven: Most of my friends I had that were living that life are gone. Two of my friends were incarcerated and both of them came home around the same time. My friend Ashante, we called him Fat Daddy or Hot Daddy, was murdered. My other friend named Spencer was called Lil Funk. He was a rapper. He was murdered also. So I'm having a lack of trust again.

Kareem: Has the transition been difficult from the street life to normal life?

Steven: The most difficult part is what people hold over your head about your past. That's why I say a lot of people are contradictions—they supposedly live these Christian values and they're supposed to have forgiveness. So, hell yeah, it's been hard.

When I came home from prison, I wound up working at a Sherwin-Williams delivering paint. I didn't check anything on my application when it asked whether I was a convicted felon. When they did the criminal background check, they found out, and fired me. I wrote the CEO a touching letter but he never responded.

I couldn't get a job for a year. It made me want to say, "F everything," and go back to the street life. The penal system says, "Okay, we'll punish you by sending you to prison but then when you come home you can't get a job, too." What do you expect people to do? What do you honestly expect people to do? People aren't going to work in McDonald's where they can't take care of themselves or their families. That's why people constantly come home and go back to the same thing.

You and I will walk through the French Quarter, and I'll show you the different people's reactions. If we have saggy pants on, people will just clutch their purses and walk totally different. And then I'll wear my glasses and be dressed up, and you'll just see people's whole demeanor change. Man, it's so crazy. Ignorance, basically.

Kareem: Where do you live now?

Steven: I'm living in Metairie. It's not the hood, definitely not. I can say that—a nice environment.

Kareem: Which colleges have you attended?

Steven: I attended Grambling State University, Louisiana Tech University, Southern University of New Orleans, and Delgado. I'm at University of New Orleans working on a degree in urban planning to give me a holistic view.

Kareem: Has college given you a different view on life?

Steven: Yeah, it preps you for life. It gives you a basis for it, but it doesn't guarantee you success. It's not for everybody. It's not really all what it seems to be.

Kareem: What do you do for fun?

Steven: For fun? I live a square life now. I like going to the bookstore, still like doing poetry, walking in the park. Anything that's simple.

Kareem: Who influences you?

Steven: Malcolm X, love that dude. All my little brothers and sisters because I gotta make a way. I still feel like it's up to me to provide for my family.

Kareem: What do you plan to accomplish in the next five years?

Steven: Finish school, gain more experience. Hopefully write a book.

Kareem: Are there any thoughts or ideas you would like to add?

Steven: I just hope that everybody can get the full blessings of the Constitution. That's my whole thing—that we all can get the same equal rights that the Constitution provides.

THE ORIGINAL
MARBLE COVER-48 Sheets

NAME _____

WIDE RULED
ROARING SPRING, PA 16673

School

I always have had a good head on my shoulders when it came to academics. The thirst and admiration for knowledge has been embedded in me since I was young. My aunt would force me to read books which I begun to explore my passion for reading. The first book that captivated my imagination and open another side of me was Harry Potter and the Socercer's Stone. I felt a connection with Harry except for the fact that my parents weren't dead. That

Interview with my Aunt, Alice Washington

Tall and graceful when she walks, my aunt is a humble soul but if you get on her bad side, she can be pretty straightforward. Growing up, she was half caretaker and half landlady.

At her house, I was always reminded of Blackness. She had small decorative statues of African men and women, and painted Afrocentric canvases. She believed that gaining an education was the only way for Black people to achieve. She occasionally talked about the art—why she chose the images—but even when she wasn't talking, the art was speaking for itself.

She would make me read and remind me that there was a time in American history when Black people didn't have the right to read. I got into the stories. The one that really stands out is Harry Potter, although I read African folktales and know they are in my brain somewhere.

One day, Aunt Alice brought a VHS tape home called Our Friend Martin, *a cartoon. She told us that we could learn a lot from this. I watched it with my little cousins, and was swept into the story about two friends who travel back in time and meet Martin Luther King, Junior. The lessons of friendship and struggle stayed with me up until now.*

Aunt Alice is one of our keepers of family history. I wanted to hear her perspective on raising so many children. Even though I moved out years ago, I stop by to holla at her and see what she's doing.

Kareem and Alice Washington, by Lindsey Darnell.

Kareem: Good evening, Aunt Alice. How are you doing?

Alice: I'm doing fine, and you?

Kareem: I'm all right. Where did you grow up?

Alice: I grew up right here in New Orleans, Louisiana. I was raised as a child in the St. Bernard Project.

Kareem: What was it like growing up in the St. Bernard?

Alice: During the 50s, it was a very good environment. It was just like being in an African village—everyone looked out for each other.

Kareem's great-grandmother Alice Garrett Scott, courtesy of Alice Washington.

Kareem: How would you describe it to someone who has never been?

Alice: I think it would be pretty hard to describe it because there are no more projects. They're a residential area now. It's definitely time for a change. Even though you had your protesters out there who were living in the 20th century when this is the 21st century.

Kareem: Do you know why your parents decided to move to the St. Bernard?

Alice: During those rough times, there were not too many places where a Black person really could go and find a decent environment to live. My father came from Mississippi. His parents died at a very young age. He's a fraternal twin with his sister. Both of their names are Abbie. One is A-B-B-I-E and the other one name is A-B-B-E-Y. They raised their siblings and sent them off to college. Right now, they're school teachers and professors, yes.

My mother, Alberta, was from Plaquemines Parish. There was no opportunity for Blacks except for maybe in the cotton field or sugarcane fields. They came to New Orleans for opportunities.

Kareem: What did they do for a living?

Alice: On my mom's side of the family, everyone was entrepreneurs. I'm trying to say it correctly. Sometimes I get twisted with the words. On that side of the family, you had an uncle. He was considered extremely rich. He went to New York City and owned the Garrett Hotel. My mother was a housekeeper, and my father, he was a printer. He worked on the edge of the French Quarter for A.F. LaBorde printing books, calendars, and so forth. They were right on Frenchmen Street.

Kareem: What do you remember most about your parents?

Alice: I can tell you they both were hard workers. Mom didn't have to work, but she chose to work because she wanted to make sure we had everything. Today, I still hear some of my generation say that they had to do without this and do without that. We never did without anything—never. They always made sure we had a decent meal. On a Monday, we had a roast with green peas while some people ate red beans.

Kareem: Are you the oldest child?

Alice: I'm the oldest child out of five.

Kareem: Can you name them?

Above: Kareem's grandmother, Alberta Scott Douglas. *Right:* Kareem's grandfather, Abbie Douglas.

Alice: Yes, I can. We'll start off with Rose, she's next in line. After that you have my brother Abbey, he's the only male of the family. Then you have Marlene and Jeanette. I'm anywhere between nine and 11 years older than them. I helped raise my siblings.

Kareem: How is your relationship with them?

Alice: It's not good. It's not good. Marlene is the only one I really keep in contact with. I enjoyed raising them, but pulled away from them later on.

Kareem: Where did you go to school?

Alice: I went to school at Carver.

Kareem: What was your favorite subject?

Alice: Being honest with you, history. I'm a person that just loves books. I read everything.

Kareem: What type of work did you do growing up?

Alice: During that time, there weren't too many opportunities. I went away to Job Corps, took up X-ray technician, and worked at Mercy Hospital for nearly five years. Then I got married. After I divorced, I inherited four of your mom's children and Jeanette's one child on top of my four. I took that type of work in order to be off on Saturdays and Sundays.

Kareem: How long did you live in the St. Bernard?

Alice: Let me tell you, I saw a change in the project. I got out of it when I was nearly 16 with my girlfriend Linda. She said, "Would you like to visit a friend in Clinton, Iowa?" and I said, "Sure, let's go." It was snowing, snowing. I always like to try something different in life. I wasn't there more than five months and after that we went to Chicago for two. I loved Chicago. I met Lou Rawls when he first started off in a small nightclub in Old Town Chicago. I met many people like Etta James out in that area, but after awhile I just wanted to come back home. Yeah, because being here is kind of slow-paced. You take your time and do everything.

After the divorce, we stayed at the St. Bernard for about six months with my mother. I got my children out of the St. Bernard and rented a house on Bruxelles Street and from there, I bought a four-plex across the street.

Kareem: What made you want to take on the responsibility of raising me and my siblings?

Alice: Because I believed I could do it and I wanted to give everyone an opportunity to move forward. You're one I'm proud of since you're going to school.

Kareem: When did you first recognize that I wasn't being taken care of properly?

Alice: When—oh Kareem, I don't want to hurt your feelings. You were only ten months old. I found you upstairs in the projects in the house by yourself. It was in October and you were naked. I picked you up and carried you home.

Kareem: What do you think is the cause of my mom's drug usage?

Alice: Well, like I said we had different generations. My generation, we call that the drug generation. The next generation was the materialistic generation. Today is the murder generation. That's the way I see it. Marlene's was peer pressure. She wanted to grow up too fast.

Kareem: Do you regret raising me and my siblings?

Alice: Never. I would never have that regret at all.

Kareem: How did you maintain control over the household?

Alice: Let's see—everyone had chores to do. Not only that, I loved to participate in school activities—football, basketball, whatever sport you were in, I tried to be there. I might not have done a good job, but I tried.

Kareem: Can you describe some of your methods of disciplining us?

Alice: Well, I'm gonna be honest with you. My way wasn't a good way at all. But since I'm older and much wiser, I'm sorry that I did it. I used to hit y'all. I don't know if it was because I was raising nine children and all the pressure was on me. So I was wrong and I definitely apologize for that. Can you forgive me?

Kareem: You're forgiven.

Alice: Okay, thanks.

Kareem: Why didn't you send me to Boys Town like my other siblings?

Alice: Because I saw more in you. And a lot of the family members had some type of drug problem. I wanted to keep everyone out of the children's lives. I was trying to get your mom to get her life straight before entering your lives. She would come by the house unannounced and sometimes she would upset y'all. It's according to how she looked, or if she was high. I did try to keep her out. Now that y'all are grown, I want you to have that relationship with your mom. I was wrong because no matter what goes on in life, you need that relationship with your parent.

Kareem: What is your most vivid memory of me?

Alice: You were no angel, okay, but I can remember when I used to be so proud of you. You were on the honor roll. You lived on the honor roll. Sometimes you got off the honor roll and I had to get on your behind.

Kareem: How would you describe me in one word?

Alice: Well, I'm gonna let you smile: Adorable.

Kareem: How is your relationship with our family now?

Alice: Well, you know Kareem, I'm still estranged from them.

Kareem: Do you think that one day our family will cooperate and let go of the past?

Alice: I'm praying for that. The only way that can happen is through prayers.

Kareem: Did living on Bruxelles make the responsibility of raising us easier?

Alice: Yes it did, much easier. Because we were homeowners, we were taking care of our property. Not only that, I didn't have to worry about

someone knocking on my door and just aggravating me. If you lived in the project, someone was always knocking on your door, "Can I borrow an egg, I'ma gonna give it back?" And you never see it. That's the way the old folks do it, okay. Not only that, it just made me go forward. Like I said, everyone on my father's side is educated, everyone on my mom's side are entrepreneurs.

Remember I made y'all do without two Christmases? I wouldn't buy any toys. I just bought the basics— the clothes, the shoes, the food. I told y'all we were going to save up and buy a house. Raising nine children in a two-bedroom house was kind of hard. I bought a fourplex and that fourplex had three bedrooms per apartment.

That wasn't my first house. That was house number five for me. My first home I owned when I was only 18 was in Marrero on Robinson Avenue and after that it was in the East on Babylon.

Kareem, second from right, in a kindergarten, courtesy of Alice Washington.

A painting of the rag man by Alice Washington. Photograph by Lindsey Darnell.

Kareem: What did you do for fun?

Alice: You know I love art. I'm working on some canvases now. I used to do portraits but since my eyesight is getting bad I went on to do oil painting. Right now I'm doing folk art and I'm going back nearly 50 plus years ago. I'll be telling my age if I tell you exactly.

I'd like to put it on eBay. Folk art definitely sells but you have to recall your memories. Right now, I'm working on a canvas and it's showing an old mule pulling a wagon. They used to have the rag man who went around the neighborhood and would pay you five cents for your used clothes.

Kareem: What is your favorite getaway spot?

Alice: Atlanta. We'll walk around the campuses at Spellman, Clark, and Morehouse. Plus, we'll go visit the Martin Luther King Museum and the mall. Plus, I get my daughter to bring me to the airport because they have beautiful artworks, sculptures. It's just like being in a museum. And I'm looking forward to going to Pike County, Arkansas to get in that dirt and dig for diamonds. I've been knowing about it for almost 20 years.

Kareem: Why is education important to you?

Alice: For me or for you?

Kareem: For you.

Alice: I just like to see young people go forward. I know I can go forward. As I tell everyone, "God gave us all a talent, but some of us don't know how to use that talent." Some have the brains for college and some need to go to a trade school, you see? It makes a big difference in life—just going forward.

TO PARENTS OR GUARDIAN:

Student success in school depends to a large extent on a cooperative relationship between home and school. You are urged to contact the school whenever there is a need for information about student progress or the school and its educational offerings.

Morris L. Holmes, Ed.D., Superintendent

Student's Name: _Kareem Kennedy_   ID#: _____   Grade: _1_

Teacher: _Dr. Davidson_

School: _Langston Hughes_

Principal: _Mrs. Richards_

Teacher: _____

School: _____

Principal: _____

COMMENTS

FIRST QUARTER: _Kareem is a smart boy and a good student._

Parent's Signature: _____

SECOND QUARTER: _Kareem is a good boy but he is playing too much and not focusing on his work._

Parent's Signature: _____

THIRD QUARTER: _____

Parent's Signature: _____

LANGUAGE	1	2	3	4	AVG.
Instructional level	B	B			
	OL	OL			
Completes classwork					
Completes homework		✓			
Expresses self well in writing	✓				
Listens attentively	✓	✓			
Takes part in discussion	✓	✓			
Uses grammar skills well	✓	✓			
Spells assigned words		✓			
Uses correct spelling in writing		✓			
Expresses self well orally	✓	✓			
Writes legibly and neatly	✓	✓			
Effort	✓	✓			

READING	1	2	3	4	AVG.
Instructional level	A	B			
	OL	OL			
Completes classwork	✓				
Completes homework		✓			
Understands what is read					
Uses word attack skills					
Reads independently	✓	✓			
Uses class and library resources		✓			
Effort					

MATHEMATICS	1	2	3	4	AVG.
Instructional level	B	B			
	OL	OL			
Completes classwork		✓			
Completes homework	✓	✓			
Understands place value		✓			
Works accurately	✓	✓			
Can read and solve word problems		✓			
Understands and uses					
Addition		✓			
Subtraction	✓	✓			
Multiplication					
Division					
Fractions/Decimals					
Measurement					
Effort	✓	✓			

SOCIAL STUDIES	1	2	3	4	AVG.
	A	B			
Completes classwork	✓	✓			
Completes homework		✓			
Works well in group projects	✓	✓			
Knows how to use books for information					
Learns necessary facts		✓			
Reads maps with understanding					
Understands current events					
Effort	✓	✓			

SCIENCE	1	2	3	4	AVG.
	B	B			
Completes classwork	✓	✓			
Completes homework	✓	✓			
Is interested in how and why	✓	✓			
Uses many books and resources	✓	✓			
Understands basic concepts	✓	✓			
Effort	✓	✓			

SECOND LANGUAGE	1	2	3	4	AVG.
Effort	—	—			

PHYSICAL EDUCATION	1	2	3	4	AVG.
Good sportsmanship	✓	✓			
Responsible for personal hygiene	✓	✓			
Observes safety practices	✓	✓			
Effort	✓	✓			

ART	1	2	3	4	AVG.
Effort	✓	✓			

MUSIC	1	2	3	4	AVG.
Band	—	—			
Classroom Music/Vocal Music	✓	✓			
Effort	✓	✓			

SOCIAL DEVELOPMENT LIVING AND WORKING TOGETHER	1	2	3	4
Follows directions	✓	✓		
Reports to class on time	✓	✓		
Has necessary materials	✓	✓		
Begins work promptly	✓	✓		
Works in orderly manner	✓	✓		
Works independently	✓	✓		
Works accurately	✓	✓		
Is dependable		✓		
Accepts responsibility for actions	✓	X		
Accepts constructive criticism	✓	X		
Observes rules and regulations	✓	X		
Takes care of materials	✓	✓		
Neat in written work	✓			
Uses time to good advantage	✓			
Demonstrates good citizenship				

	1	2	3	4	AVG.
Average of Promotional Subjects	A	B			
Behavior	B	C			

RECORD OF ATTENDANCE

QUARTER	1	2	3	4	TOTAL
Days in Period	44	44			
Days Present	43	42			
Days Absent	1	2			
Days Tardy	0	0			
Late Entry Date					

After careful consideration, we feel that _____

will profit most by working in grade _____ in fall, 19_____.

Teacher's Signature

Principal's Signature

EVALUATION KEY
A - 93 - 100 - Superior
B - 85 - 92 - Above Average
C - 75 - 84 - Average
D - 70 - 74 - Limited Progress
F - 60 - 69 - Failure

INSTRUCTIONAL LEVEL KEY
AL - Above Level
OL - On Level
RL - Remedial Level

SUB-ITEMS KEY
✓ - Making Progress
X - Needs Improvement
— - Not Applicable

White - Teacher's Record   Green - 4th Quarter   Yellow - 3rd Quarter   Pink - 2nd Quarter   Goldenrod - 1st Quarter

Kareem's first grade report card, courtesy of Kareem Kennedy.

First Grade

In Dr. Davidson's class at Langston Hughes Elementary, we learned how a caterpillar gets its wings and how to observe the bugs in our environment. On the first day, my neighbor from around the block, Jessica, came into class. Some people called her a white girl and I clipped one guy who decided to join in. The whole school had virtually all dark-skinned kids. She wasn't one to rebel, so I guess she got used to the name calling. She lived around the corner from my aunt with her father. Aunt Alice knew Mr. Andy, her dad, who was white and worked as a painter and Jessica would sometimes come by our house to wait for him to get off work. She used to call me cousin, and said, "Thanks for sticking up for me."

When school was out for the day, the school bus was waiting outside to pick us up. One day, I had to use the bathroom just before the final bell. I told Dr. Davidson, "I got to use it." He denied my request. When the bell rang, I wanted to maneuver to the restroom, but I knew the buses didn't wait for people. I decided to wait until I made it home. My bus, No. 64, was one of the rowdiest around the neighborhood. We would chant and bang on the aluminum roof, "64 gonna bust yo nose! Oh! Oh!" and, "Yo mama, yo daddy: Leave that crack alone!" I usually joined in unison but all I could think about was the toilet. As we passed St. Leo the Great, a Catholic school just outside the neighborhood, everyone began to chant, "St. Leo Fake! Oh! Oh!"

My stomach began to churn. I tried to hold it but a tingling feeling came over me and out it came.

Langston Hughes Elementary, by Kareem Kennedy.

Luckily, I had a seat to myself. I put my head down thinking, "I'm going to be the joke of the year." About a block away from my stop, a kid named Vernon, who was sitting in the seat in front of me, said, "Man, who that is smelling like a dumpster!" Before I could be found out, the bus pulled up to the last stop, which was mine. I fumbled around with my backpack and let the other kids go first—then made my slow exit off the bus.

I told Aunt Alice what happened. She said, "Next time, if he won't let you use the bathroom, just walk out, and I'll deal with Dr. Davidson." I felt relieved because I thought I did something wrong. Dr. Davidson kept a piece of a thick branch, about the length of a baseball bat that looked as if ants carved it. If you got caught goofing off, he would give you a sharp tap to the noggin causing you not only pain, but laughter from classmates. He would get into these speeches about metamorphosis and have us look at our surroundings, which got boring when recess approached.

Second Grade

St. Louis Cemetery No. 2, by Kareem Kennedy.

Aunt Alice told me, "Your mom sent you something." I took the letter into my bedroom to open it. I knew her handwriting: straight and clear cursive. It was an orange and purple card made with construction paper at St. Gabriel's Women's prison. On the front she had written, "Happy Birthday, Son! I love you."

My birthday was on Halloween so I didn't get many other gifts—only candy from trick–or–treating. I like how it's the first major holiday after Mardi Gras that calls for a party. The weather cools down and people have better attitudes. I've always been an observer gathering information so I appreciated having my birthday on a day when it was expected for people to come out of their shells.

My auntie told me she dressed me up as Barney the dinosaur one time, but I'm glad I don't remember it. Most of the time, my best friend Mario and I would just walk around in regular clothes while Alice sat on the porch passing out candy.

I got looks from people when I told them my birthday was on Halloween. My friends teased me, calling me the Devil's Son, and even my teachers were superstitious. In school, we learned that the day after my birthday was All Saint's Day when people whitewashed the tombs to pay homage to the dead. My family didn't have many deaths and so I never got to see how to pay respect. But I used to pass the cemeteries walking down Esplanade or North Claiborne—they were raggedy, but had the potential to be beautiful. Now when I pass them, I tap my chest twice with my fist, once for life and once for death.

Aunt Rose's church, by Kareem Kennedy.

Third Grade

I never really cared too much about church, but I often found myself in service clapping and singing in the pews. When people asked, "What is your religion?" I told them, "I have none."

I started out going to church with my Aunt Rose. I liked bible study because afterwards they gave us juice and cookies. Services were too boring for me to handle, so I started to avoid my aunt and the church van by pretending to be in a coma until they had passed by my Aunt Alice's house.

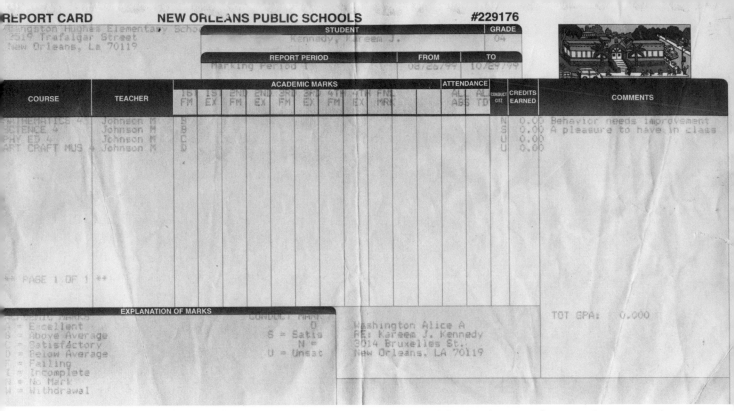

Kareem's fourth grade report card, courtesy of Kareem Kennedy.

Fourth Grade

The state started doing standardized testing and all fourth graders had to take the LEAP test. I had Mr. Taylor—a young black man who wore glasses and had pencil-sized dreadlocks. Mario and me were in the same class that year. He mostly worshipped his girlfriend who always made him mad. I was known for being the best speller in the class—the last one left standing in the spelling bee.

In the middle of that year, Mr. Taylor told us we were going to be given a test. If we didn't score at basic or higher we wouldn't be promoted to fifth grade. None of us cared about taking the test. We never had to take one before that mattered. He said it would be based on what we learned in Social Studies, Math, English, and Science.

I had gotten kicked out of school for fighting. Mr. Taylor told me I had potential but it was my fourth suspension of the year, which caused expulsion. Aunt Alice was mad and tried to make me keep up with my classes during the day while she was at work. Instead I explored the house, snooping around in places I knew I wasn't allowed to go, and playing the Hot Boyz loud on the surround sound.

Around the near-end of the school year, I had to come into school and take the LEAP test. When I looked at the test, it seemed as if it were in Spanish and I regretted putting the Hot Boyz before my studying.

Towards the end of the school year, a piece of mail came for me while Aunt Alice wasn't home. I opened up my LEAP scores and they all read

"Unsatisfactory." At the bottom it said, "Your child will not be promoted to the next grade." A flyer for summer school was attached. My aunt never saw the mail. It was well hidden.

My aunt was a busy person who seldom had time to check on my school life. I told all my friends I passed, and they all told me they had to go to summer school. After I was let off punishment, I ignored my failing and enjoyed the rest of the summer on Bruxelles, getting in water fights and playing basketball and football.

On the first day of the following year, a list with everyone's name, grade, and teacher was posted on the walls of the front entrance. I scanned the list for my name on the fifth grade posters. I saw a couple of my friends' names and looked for my best friend Mario's name because his always came right after mine on the roll.

I saw Mario's name on Mr. Payton's fifth grade class list, but mine wasn't there. I looked at the other fifth grade class—it wasn't there either. With a feeling of dread, I looked over on the fourth grade poster and saw "Kareem Kennedy" listed under Mr. Taylor's class. I felt stupid, maybe even a little humiliated, because I been in denial all summer. I had to psych myself up to come to the conclusion: Work extra hard to redeem myself.

Everything went smoothly until my first quarter report card conference. The school called home to notify parents of Report Card Night.

I went with Aunt Alice after she got off work. We headed down the hall for my class, and Mr. Taylor stood in the door. He said, "Good evening, Ms. Washington. Hey, Mr. Kennedy. I think you're on the right road this year." I looked up and said, "Yup."

My aunt told him that we were coming to get my report card. He told her that I was the last student he was waiting on. She asked him, "Oh, you teach fifth grade now?" I looked down.

He said, "No, I'm still hanging in there with fourth grade." My aunt figured things out pretty quickly, saying, "Kareem, what grade are you in?"

Interview with My Best Friend, Jurand "Mario" Louis

My ace, compadre, right hand man, brother from another, Mario has been a part of my life since pitch up tackle. Slim and tall, dark, with a head full of locks, stands Mario.

I first met him when I used to walk to D&M Store and he would be sitting on the steps of the fourplex where he, his mother, older brother, Durand, and two younger twin brothers, Branden and Bradley, lived. Mario and I walked to school when were young, talking about the Saints, girls, problems with family. Mario was the athletic type who always played sports. I played sometimes, but I was more of an analyst, watching on.

Kareem: What's up, Mario?

Mario: What's up?

Kareem: How you feeling?

Mario: All right. Still living.

Kareem: What part of the Seventh Ward are you from?

Mario: Bruxelles Street.

Kareem: How would you describe it for someone who hasn't been there before?

Mario: A nice neighborhood off Paris Avenue, Gentilly. Family oriented.

Kareem: How long have you lived in the Seventh Ward?

Mario: 15 years of my life.

Photographs of Mario on Bruxelles, by Kareem Kennedy.

Kareem: What is your relationship like between Bruxelles and St. Bernard?

Mario: A lot of people move off of Bruxelles into the St. Bernard, and a lot of people move out of the St. Bernard onto Bruxelles. I have family from the St. Bernard—my father and his children, my little brothers.

Kareem: There's a connection cause it's so close—the neighborhood and the project are right there. How did your parents make a living?

Mario: My mom worked two jobs: the Sheraton at least ten years and she worked at a grocery store. She started at the bottom, worked her way up to the top. She was working in housekeeping for plenty of years. Then she moved to the front desk and is now a supervisor over the front desk. My father, he was what they call an entrepreneur.

Kareem: Hood entrepreneur?

Mario: A hood entrepreneur.

Kareem: What is it like to have little brothers who are twins—Branden and Bradley?

Mario: When you get into it with one, you got to get into it with both of them.

Kareem: How can you tell the difference?

Mario: I've been around them so long, they don't look alike to me. One is bigger than the other one.

Kareem: How did you get your nickname?

Mario: Well, my mama's close friend's name is Mario and she called me after him. He's cool. You would think he's my father, but he's not. He stays on Bruxelles to this day.

Kareem: Always washing his car every Sunday. What is our relationship?

Mario: We met in fourth grade. We're like brothers. Not friends, more like brothers.

Kareem: Can you tell me a time when we really click clacked and made a bond?

Mario: Oh, man, I don't know—there were so many. We've just done everything together. Everywhere you were, I was.

Kareem: I know one, but it was bad. We were knuckleheads. Being poor, too, we didn't have that much so sometimes we went into Dillard's and stole clothes. Whenever I had, you had. Whenever you had, I had. It's like that. I had a bad temper.

Mario: Couldn't tell you nothing.

Kareem: You were the funny guy. And you helped me with all my tough fights.

Mario: I know one story when you were fighting a dude with a cast. My brothers came running home, "Oh, Kareem's fighting!" I went down there and you were fighting a dude with one arm.

Kareem: I don't mention this too much, but he actually got the best of me cause he had that cast on. He busted me up in the nose. You saved me that day.

Mario: I'm really a quiet fella. A calm and collected person. But when you hit that button, I'm like a whole other person. That's how my dad was—quiet. He'd joke a lot, but you hit that button, and you'd feel his wrath.

Kareem: Will you talk about the famous pickup basketball games on Bruxelles? AKA the corner?

Mario: I was like the best they ever had. I was like a street legend. My father was into sports, but the streets took him. He didn't want the same for me. He wanted me to play basketball. When I lost him, I continued playing, but the streets just took me in and I lost it. I had another partner out of the Seventh Ward Bruxelles. Thomas was a nice basketball player. He got killed.

Kareem: Thomas, yeah. We call him Ray. He taught me how to be silly, how to be more down to earth. He also motivated me to start college cause I used to see him on Canal Street, getting out of work at McDonald's with his work uniform still on. I'd ask him, "Where you going, Ray?"

"I'm about to go to class." He motivated me.

Kareem: What was your dad like?

Mario: He was loving. He was strict. He was doing wrong, but he didn't want to see his children do anything wrong. Stay in school. He took me to play basketball on Saturdays outside the project. If I missed a shot, I had to run around the court. I was out there sweating, working hard. I know if my father would still be here, I'd be in somebody's college playing basketball on a T.V. somewhere—guaranteed.

Kareem: Is that where you got your jump shot from?

Mario: My father had a nice thick scrapbook with newspaper articles, but he messed up and dropped out in the twelfth grade. Didn't graduate. My uncle was telling me that during one game a scout for Nichols State was there for him. His team was losing and the coach took him out of the game. He just exploded—kicking chairs and all that. It was crazy.

Kareem: You got to tell about mom.

Mario: She stayed on us hard. You would come knocking on the door, *don don don*, early in the morning, and she would scream, "Get away from my door. They punished." She punished us a lot—she didn't play. She's a strong Black woman. She raised four boys by herself. She worked two jobs. Talk about times when I didn't see my mom in four days and we stayed in the same house! I'm at school, she's at work. By the time we'd make it home, she'd be gone to her next job.

Kareem: Ms. Tracy was like a real step-mom to me. Like a mother that I never really had. Wherever you went, I was right there—second lines, the mall. I love her cooking.

Mario: Jambalaya, that's her dish.

Mario as a young boy, courtesy of the Louis family.

Kareem: Has the death of your father changed your attitude on life?

Mario: Really, yes, cause when he died I was like, "What I'm living for?" He was my everything. I didn't spend time with him every day cause he was in the streets hustling. When I did get time, I cherished it. I didn't know when the next time was going to be.

He got killed right there on Ursulines and North Robertson in the Sixth Ward. He got killed in front of Joe's Cozy Corner. A month after my birthday. I had just made 12 years old. My birthday was in September, and we hung out at a second line in the same spot he got killed.

He must have known he was going to get killed. Every birthday, he used to give me a little money. This year, he took me out to eat, took me to the second line, bought me clothes, put money in my pocket. He knew it was his time.

Kareem: How has it been for your family?

Mario: It's been hard. My brothers don't listen to my mom a lot. All my mom had to do before was pick up the phone, and he was coming. Everybody in the house was scared. He was tough, strict.

Kareem: Will you tell about your tattoo?

Mario: This one is "M&M" for my father. His name was Lionel Mason. And this one is half of a heart. My girlfriend has the other half.

Kareeem: How long have you been growing your dreadlocks and what do they represent to you?

Mario: I've been growing them for four years, and to me, they represent the struggles we've been through.

Kareem: Do you get harassed by the police for your hair?

Mario: Yeah, and you get discriminated by a lot of people. A lot of people think cause you have dreads, "Oh, you just a hoodlum."

Kareem: Do people think that you're a weed-head for having dreadlocks?

Mario: There's a lot of people who think, "Oh, he got dreads—oh, he smoke." Automatic. The job I'm working at now, I went and filled out an application. The man, he didn't call me right back, but I kept call-ing him, kept calling him, and I got on. Now, we're cool, but he came out like a man and told me, "When you first came, I seen them dreads. You know what I'm saying? People stereotype y'all for that."

Kareem: Why did you stay for Katrina?

Mario: Well, we really wanted to leave but we didn't have the funds. Before Katrina, I was at Abramson. We had just moved out to the East about six months before. We got a free room at the Sheraton where my mom works, so we just stayed in the hotel.

Kareem: Where did you go afterwards?

Mario: We went to Dallas, Texas. My auntie had been wanting me to move to Houston before Katrina, so she came and picked me up from Dallas. I moved to Houston at the beginning of my 11th grade year.

Kareem: Was it hard for you to adjust to the school?

Mario: Yeah, it was hard cause they were teaching stuff in Texas that we weren't even learning down here. It was a nice experience to expand your mind. It was a fresh start for me. And I was playing bas-ketball until they told me I had to cut off my hair to continue playing. And by transferring from New Orleans to Texas, I didn't have enough credits. I told my mama, "I'm ready to go back home." She was like, "Everybody in the house ready to go back except for me." I guess we over-voted her.

Kareem: Where did you move, after the storm when you came back?

Mario: We moved back into the East in an apart-ment in the Willows.

Kareem: How does the East compare to the Seventh Ward?

Mario: Well, before Katrina, we really couldn't hang outside with our friends. We were staying in apartment complex, and it really was boring. I used to catch the bus to the Seventh Ward and come home late.

Kareem: What was it like to try to get back to school after the storm?

Mario: After the storm, it was hard to get back to school. All the schools were really full so I had to go to Frederick Douglas in the Ninth Ward. When they were teaching us, I was like, "Man, I already know all this. I learned this in Houston." It was a piece of cake.

Kareem: What kind of music do you like?

Mario: Rap. I like Jay–Z, the whole Roc-A-Fella. I like the Hot Boyz. Soulja Slim, B.G. They come from out the struggle. B.G.'s life pertains to mine. He was close to his father and lost him at a young age. His birthday is on the same day as my birthday. He grew up in the neighborhood, ran through the projects.

I like any rapper who raps about the streets. Lil Wayne—he's all right, but what he raps about doesn't pertain to my lifestyle. A lot of people rap about it, but don't really live it.

Kareem: What you call studio gangstas.

Mario: You can really feel when they're coming from their soul. You can only pretend for so long.

Kareem: Do you still communicate with your little brothers on your dad's side?

Mario: Yeah, I communicate with all of them. I'm trying to get my money right where I can get a car, so I can get all my brothers and sisters together so we can take a family portrait and give one to our grandma for Christmas. The twins are with my mom in the East. I got a big brother who stays uptown with his girlfriend and son. Two little brothers with different mamas who stay in different parts of Atlanta. I have a little sister staying in the Lower Ninth Ward, and another sister staying in Houston, Texas.

Kareem: Where do you see yourself in the next five years?

Mario: I see myself finishing up school in sports management, getting my degree, coaching. I'd like to have a nice house in LaPlace, Metairie, or somewhere further out the way. See myself with my girlfriend, nice car, and one child. I'll always visit the Seventh Ward, but at the end of the day, I'm going home. They got a lot of people that just hate. I saw how they hated on my daddy. So why would I live in the Seventh Ward with my family and my wife and put their life at risk?

In five years, hopefully have me an album dropped. Before the hurricane, I used to write my raps. A lot of people say, "Oh man, who that is? Who you stealing from?" And I'm not stealing, it just sounds that good—I'm like the black superman without the cape.

Fifth Grade

Bruxelles was a narrow street about six blocks long with McDonald's at the North and Popeye's to the South. In between, the street was lined with fourplexes and double shotgun houses. Before the storm, many teenagers and small children used to call them home. It also had its fair share of elderly residents like Ms. Daisy, the woman who you always saw sitting on her porch or taking a walk down the block. Papa Henry, who used to ask me to walk to the store to get a pack of his favorite cigarettes, Pall Mall Reds, was a real Bruxelles veteran.

During the week, Aunt Alice made me stay inside to get my studies done. On the weekends, I used to kick it with the neighborhood kids. Brian lived down the block between Abundance and Agriculture. He stayed upstairs in a fourplex with his mom, stepdad and brother Chris. I remember Chris well because he was a comedian and got around in a wheel chair. Everyone knew him by his loud mouth and jokes. He had a sickness that paralyzed his legs. He died when he was 13 from natural causes and everyone from the hood attended the funeral.

On the corner of Bruxelles and Abundance, you used to catch the HBL (Hood Basketball League) after school and on weekends. The corner wasn't an extravagant gym, but for us it was all that was needed—a basketball goal, ball players, water, and hustle energy. The goal was stored in Brian's backyard. Everyone would hang on the steps of the fourplex before we rolled the goal and tire to the corner.

Countless summers were spent on that corner—three-on-three's, dunk contests, three-point shoot-outs—a hood arena. Out-of-bounds was the sidewalk or behind the street drains. The crowd was people from the neighborhood, and time-out came when a car passed and we would say, "Car time!" After the game, we had Comedy Central on Brian's steps, ribbing each other until all of us were crying and laughing.

The main players who balled on the regular were: Brian, Juggie, Mario, Thomas, Dexter, Marlon, Durand, Ray, Tall Dwayne, Ben, and Merlin. Brian was known for his Dirk Nowitzki type of ball play. He didn't have quick moves but had mega range. Juggie was known for his handles with the ball—he was like a young Chauncey Billups. My homie Ray played possessed. He was a defensive machine hustling for rebounds, and saving loose balls. Marlon went to St. Augustine High, an all-boys school. I guess they taught him discipline because you never caught Marlon without a ball. He went on to play in college. Sometimes other hoods would put together a team and try to take down our corner, which rarely happened.

When Brian wasn't home and we needed to get the goal, we had to ask Brian's grandpa, who lived next door. We took turns asking permission because of his grandpa's love of cats. As you walked up the steps, you saw about two dozen cats lounging like they owned the place. The closer we got to the front door, the more cats you saw lifting the tails, marking their territories. When you made it to the door and knocked he would take a nice minute to reach it, and then say, "Wassup young fellas?" "Just cooling." We'd ask for the goal and he'd point to the yard and say, "Go ahead, bring it back when you're finished."

The corner wasn't always an oasis. As the temperature went up so did tempers, which sometimes led to summertime scuffles. Fights over tough fouls, the score, or just the heat causing short–fused reactions. Mr. Frank, the car repair/sweetshop man, would turn on the fire hydrant after games to cool us off.

One day, Brian, Mario, Durand, a bunch of other

people, and I were running a three-on-three. I saw Brian put his Gameboy in the mailbox across the street from where we were ballin. In my head, I weighed the options of taking the Gameboy—taking it and making me happy, taking it and making Brian sad. When Brian wasn't paying attention, I made the Gameboy vanish.

When he finally realized what took place I had already put it in my secret hiding spot. Brian went haywire when he couldn't determine who took it. He told his mother what had happened, and that seemed to be the end of it.

For one week, I played *Pokemon Red*. Slick as grease, I gamed out when no one was looking until the end of the week came. Friday, to be exact. I got caught slipping when I left the Gameboy unattended on the dresser while using the restroom. My aunt's pay-attention-to-everything sensory seized the game. I came out of the restroom just as a jolly as a rabbit. Without a warning, she snatched me up by the collar and herded me to the living room cursing and shouting. She knew it wasn't mine and whipped a confession out of me. I started off tough. I told her I got it from friend who let me borrow it. She torn down that lie like a bulldozer and whipped me some more. I couldn't take the pain any longer. I spilled the beans. Crying and angry, my aunt told me, "Don't move until I come back."

The Corner, by Kareem Kennedy.

Brian, his mom, and my aunt were all standing around me like a conference. My aunt made me apologize to Brian and his mom. After they left, Alice told me that she would buy me things if I started doing well in school. Punished the rest of the summer, I learned the message she preached to me: Thou Shall Not Steal.

Sixth Grade

For years, I had often found myself being walked to Mr. Reilhmann's class after brain wrestling (i.e. talking back) to another teacher. Mr. Reilhmann would sit me in the back of his classroom and put a volume of the *World Book* encyclopedia in front of me. He made me copy pages exactly as they were printed in the book.

If I was in his class on Friday afternoon, my punishment became enjoyable when Reilhmann would host a Jeopardy game for the students in his class to demonstrate what they learned during the week. I'd

never seen kids this hyped—clapping for joy when their table got an answer right and throwing fits when a member got one wrong.

When I was officially in his class for sixth grade, I got to experience it myself. He would give us reading, math, and social studies notes for the week. We had to learn the material in preparation for his Friday afternoon show. Whatever tables came in first place and second place received a small bundle of candy.

Mr. Reilhmann had team captains and let them choose their teams. I'd get upset sometimes when

Langston Hughes Elementary by Kareem Kennedy.

I was chosen for teams that were coming in last. I started looking for classmates who were about their business when it was time for Jeopardy.

Now that I think hard on Reilhmann's motive, I have come to the conclusion that it was an attempt to challenge our minds and get us working in unison. The sixth graders were the leaders of the school, and we had to work together at other times during the year for Christmas plays, assemblies, and Black History Month.

He was passionate about Langston Hughes, teaching us his poems and life history. We learned that Hughes was part of the Harlem Renaissance and wrote poems that gave glimpses through the eyes of a Black man. He painted brilliant pictures that brought me through time. For the Black History assembly, our class performed "A Dream Deferred" and "The Negro Speaks" in unison, leaving the audience in applause. I knew the lines practically by heart, and still do.

Seventh Grade

Gregory Junior High in the Seventh Ward was a semi-smart school—it had its patches of cultivated gardens and untended weeds. The school was divided into cadres: red and green for the seventh grade; blue and gold for the eighth grade; and purple for the ninth grade. The green cadre in the seventh was supposedly designed for the smart students while the red cadre was designated for your uncontrollable and academically challenged students. The same for eighth grade. The gold cadre students were ripe apples from the green cadre and the blue were the toughened adolescents from the red. In simple man's terms, it was sort of like a "get it where you fit in" school. Even back then, I chose friends wisely because I hated being the brand name. I like to be behind the scenes of everything. But if anyone tried something, I would turn into the Tazmanian devil of destruction. In middle school, you never knew when you could become the hunted.

Kids have statuses that are sacred to them and must be well maintained. The average kids had a status of

Photographs of Gregory, by Kareem Kennedy.

46

being cool, funny, or downright disrespectful. Nice shoes and designer clothes their parents bought made them act nonchalant. Not me. The role I played was the aggravating poor kid from the hood—smart with a real temper problem. The simple fact that I spoke my mind got me in trouble, and the fact that I never backed down from a fight kept me on the disciplinary seesaw of suspension and expulsion.

Anyway, Quinton from the red cadre was supposed to be some kind of big shot on campus. He and the clowns he ran with were known for fighting, and for just being assholes. One day at lunch everyone was standing outside the auditorium. Quinton and his friends were running around the school slapping unsuspecting weaklings from the green cadre on the back of the neck. He went around the campus and slapped a braced-faced, fat kid who just stood there—deer in the headlights. They looked like a pack of hyenas terrorizing people and Quinton snickered like a mad scientist drunk off of bullying.

Quinton decided that I would be their next victim and sent one of his boys to come do the job. I was standing along the breezeway of the auditorium and he started towards me with his hands in pocket and head lowered. He picked his head up and looked into my eyes, which were beaming with rage. He made quick eye contact and walked back towards Quinton. I took off my school bag and pulled my shirt out of my pants. Quinton tried to rush me and I backed up quickly as he swung. We managed to get to the grass in the courtyard.

My classmates gathered around us like a rowdy boxing crowd. Everything was in slow motion. I punched him and he fell. After dealing with Quinton, I didn't have to belong to any group, or wear the latest tennis shoes. I had beaten up the bully, and got respect.

Eighth Grade

A few relatives and friends gathered at a neighbor's house watching the Super Bowl between the Rams and Titans. Ganja smoke filled the air as the game went on—it was like being in a fog except inside. I watched them—how they seemed to look relaxed and very goofy. Finally, someone said, "You want this, bruh?"

Before this day, I was very uninterested in drugs, watching older cats getting blisted while in their company without wanting to try it. I don't know if it was the peer pressure or just curiosity that came over me that day, but I grabbed the blunt and put it between my lips like I was a pro. I took a hard drag, and immediately responded with an uncontrollable cough. Everyone in the room laughed and told me I had baby lungs. I took another, softer drag then passed it back. My friend glanced at the lit ganja and said "Damn, n****" you wet the 'gar!" He pulled out a lighter and danced the flame over the tip then took a hit and said, "That's how you get high!" with smoke shooting out his nose.

My relative told me, "That's enough for you." I sat back and watched the game, frequently breaking out in uncontrollable laughter when the simplest thing was said. In the fourth quarter, when the Titans marched to the end zone for a game-winning touchdown but missed by a yard, I started laughing again. My relative took me back to my aunt's house, where I immediately went to bed to hide the fun I had.

I started smoking with my friend Blo on the way to school, and then we got bold one time and decided to skip second lunch with our friend Roy to have a smoke out behind the school. We usually headed out

Promotions of a clean, healthy lifestyle at Gregory, by Kareem Kennedy.

just past the baseball field to a small wooded area that gave us a view where we could see who's coming. We were being lazy not going to the usual spot and opted for the back of the main building.

Before our lunch was over, we made it to the spot, undetected. Blo pulled out of his pockets a balled up piece of paper with a small amount of weed and asked me, "Where the 'gar?" I gave him a smashed Keep Moving that I kept inside of my binder pocket. Roy wasn't a real smoker, but didn't mind ditching Spanish class for school house adventure.

Blo stood up rolling the blunt while Roy and I traded insane ghetto stories. He said, "Man, my block so hot you could fry an egg. Ever since that the people been riding, it's so real on my way walking to the bus stop I got hacked up." I added, "Slack and

Slim was on the backstreet sitting in their car as if they were on a stakeout or something."

Blo interrupted, lighting the blunt, I chanted, "I get high, high!" We took turns on the watch post, while two of us squatted and one rotated being our eyes. Just as we're switching positions with Blo standing up, we heard a sudden crunch of fall leaves.

Brian took off. A split second later, Officer Cotton walked right past Roy and me, probably because we were in between two walls. That was our cue to break camp, running full speed out of trouble with our hearts jumping out of our chests. We went in opposite directions: Roy made his way to the gym, where everyone blended together on the old basketball court, while I maneuvered into the storage room next to the computer lab—where I hid until the school day was done.

I dozed off on top of a small file cabinet, then suddenly jumped up to the sound of a PA speaker with the voice of Mr Dupuy: "Brian Pierre, please come to the principal's office." I was surprised that it wasn't my name being called.

The final bell rung at last, but before coming out, I let the chatter of my peers disappear, then made my way to the bus stop where we met up after school. Roy was waiting there with a smirk on his face like, "Yeah, we did that." We asked the same question simultaneously, "Where's Blo?" "Man, you heard them call him on the intercom," Roy said. "I hope he ain't got popped."

We waited at the stop for five minutes, then saw Brian walking in the distance. When he reached us, he hid a big smile behind his hands. "You know I got off that. They did a CSI report to catch me, but they ain't get shit. Cotton got my name off that quiz paper I used to break the pine down. Depuy tripped my head out when he called my name, but without the evidence, them clowns ain't had nothing on me. They both tried to get me to give up y'alls names—I didn't fold."

Brian ended up getting demerits for class cutting, and a Saturday detention. The year went by with us walking on eggshells and Officer Cotton and Officer Hill keeping a close eye on each of us.

But as the school year went past, I began to notice that several of my peers kept asking, "Where the pine at?" I shrugged at their proposals, saying, "Y'all gotta get your own."

Ninth Grade

As far back as I can remember, D&M Grocery Store has been standing on the corner of Broad and Duels Street. Once painted peach, it is operated by two brothers, Danny and Mike, of Arab descent. They have repainted it many times since. When I was younger, Aunt Alice would frequently send me to the store to buy house items to cook with and two liters of Coca-Cola. My aunt was a well-known customer who bought cigarettes from D&M. When she needed a fresh deck of Capri 100's, she would call up the store and let them know I was coming in place of her. Once I gave them money, Danny would place the cigarettes in a brown paper bag and say, "Boss man, don't open it until you make it home."

The store is usually busy during the week except Sundays when everyone is watching the Saints. You can see young guys slinging dope on the corner trying to be hood rich. Bootleggers offering the latest CDs and DVDs out for a deal that usually was three for ten or five for 20. The police sometimes strolled through and shut down activity around the store. They might frisk a couple of folks and run their names in the computer to determine if any warrants were issued. Some people felt that the store was a perpetrator of violence, drugs, and alcohol. I think Danny and Mike just wanted to make some money to feed their families. I used to always buy a hot sausage on a bun with fries and a Big Shot pineapple cold drink.

I never went on the set to score weed, but I was getting small packages of smoke from a dealer who lived in the project. He was in his late teens, which meant he probably didn't care that my boys and I went to school. He just wanted the dough. That

Aunt Alice with her daughter Shawna and husband Lloyd Washington, courtesy of Alice Washington.

worked to my advantage because a lot of the older dealers knew my family and wouldn't sell to me on the strength of that. Pick-pocketing from Walgreen's candy aisle and then reselling it to customers at elementary school was my only experience in sales. When Jazz Fest came around, sometimes you could find me and Mario near the entrance with a cooler, trying to profit off bottled water, or even parking cars on property we didn't own. But I had never sold drugs.

Soon, however, I was in command of small drug enterprise. It wasn't a Fortune 500 company, but a couple of hundreds kept me satisfied. I sold at Gregory to only a select portion of the student body, which kept the heat down. My aunt had no idea what I was doing. She would have committed a homicide if she knew.

Around the same time, her husband, a pastor named Lloyd, bought the small building on the corner of Bruxelles and Treasure. Back in the day, the owners used it as a club space. A lot of violence occurred on that corner so my aunt and a bunch of neighbors signed a petition to get rid of it. After that, I think it was some kind of tax place. When my uncle bought the building, he decided to open a community grocery store. It took a while to get things together, but after a few months the store opened in the front section of the building. My uncle was invested in church so he gave the store the name Morning Glory. On opening day, the whole neighborhood came steadily to check out the business. The kids especially liked it because all the other stores were on the main streets. Kids and grown ups came for the donuts my uncle hand delivered in the morning.

In the same building, he rented out space to a dancing school and the other side became Ms. Kim and Ms. Roz's hair salon. In the rear, he created apartment space to rent. He let me make a couple of dollars here and there. I maintained the outside landscape—cut the grass, made sure trash was picked up, and passed out flyers.

But the work wasn't steady and the money wasn't always there so I kept my own enterprise going until I got arrested and expelled in the ninth grade. Aunt Alice felt let down. She said, "You're following the same path as other people in your family even after I tried to keep you away from it."

I was sent to City Youth Correctional Facility—a juvenile detention center inside of the adult prison. After a week of sitting there, I found out that parents could sign children out. I guess Aunt Alice wanted me to learn another lesson.

After I was discharged, the only educational outlet for me was the Urban League Alternative School. But the paperwork was too much for Aunt Alice who had to take time from work every time the school needed anything. I ended up sitting out the rest of the school year.

I was at home everyday, watching TV and getting on my aunt's nerves. Every day she fussed saying, "Lil boy, you're running up my pressure." She told me she couldn't raise me anymore and called me unappreciative. At the end of the year, I went back to Gregory to get my teachers to submit the grades I would have received if I hadn't got expelled. They all gave me good wishes and good marks, and as I result I didn't lose the year.

Over the summer, I had to register for a drug rehabilitation program. Although Aunt Alice took me to the program, she was frustrated and fed up with my mistakes and aggravations. She talked to her son John, and he agreed to let me come live with him in an apartment complex in New Orleans East.

He had a one-bedroom unit and gave me the living room. He was a truck driver, and was gone for long stretches of time. He paid all the rent, and made sure there was food in the fridge, but I was required to do more for myself because he was away so much. He showed me how to cook little meals for myself, like Zatarain's and rice, and baked chicken. He bought a George Forman grill to help me keep up with the times. My company was the X-Box or my friends over the phone. When I started high school, he encouraged me to graduate and join the army. He had run-ins with the law and decided to drive trucks to get out the hood. I think John likes driving because on the road, he is boss and doesn't answer to anyone.

Tenth Grade

Gregory was a feeder school to the K. The school was named after the president who helped promote civil rights, but it was still segregated. Inside the school, there were divisions as well. The hallways used to be designated unofficially by cliques, which were from different sections of the city. They had a hallway for the 17th, Gentilly, Uptown, Ninth Ward, Lafitte, and the St. Bernard. The St. Bernard was the most notorious hall, known through the school. You could easily be slapped on the back of the neck on a beautiful morning by the St. Bernard gangs. Anyone who dared to protest would be swarmed by heavy hands and hard shoes to the body.

I played everything neutral. I didn't have a crew because I didn't want to be branded like cattle. Being told what to do or having a leader doesn't sit well on my skull, but I had many allies who safeguarded me against the drama.

Uniforms were Dickies and white shirts for the fellas. The girls wore white blouses and dark blue plaid pants with thin red seams. Beyond the basics, John F. Kennedy High, aka the "K," was known for glamorous girls and guys vaunting gangsta personas. The school was given the nickname "The Fashion Show" because the students' apparel was always the latest. Jordans, G-Nikes, Hurachis, Prada, Cole Haan, and Timberland boots were all the rage.

The K was also notorious for schoolyard brawls started from wards beefing over petty stuff. On my second day of school I found out about them when

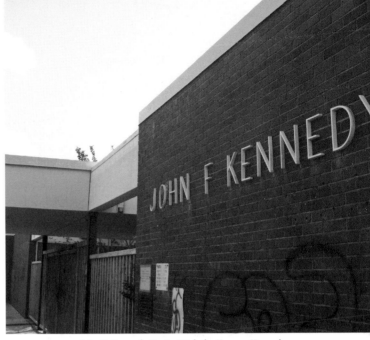

John F. Kennedy Senior High, by Kareem Kennedy.

tension arose between students from the 17th Ward and students from Gentilly. One of the Big Dogs from the 17th bumped someone from Gentilly and he went back and told his Big Dog. That started the ruckus. The student body circled around the melee—it was like watching WWF Raw, live in school.

When situations like this occurred, the crowd incited each others' fighters to unleash the pain. The brawls lasted less than ten minutes, but felt like an eternity. Staff and guards were reluctant to break up gang fights for fear of getting their heads punched. The other kids looked forward to the fights because they broke up the monotony of the day. This time, my lil partner got beaten-up slick side and was expelled.

I only went to Kennedy for two weeks when Katrina hit. My first high school got washed away in the flood. During the storm, I stayed in the Seventh Ward, going back and forth between the St. Bernard and Broad Street in a canoe I took from a neighbor.

My friend Ronald and I were waiting it out. We kept telling ourselves that the water was going down and he didn't want to leave his pit bull, Sandals. After four or five days, we finally left, hiding Sandals in a pillowcase. We were sent on a bus to Houston, where we ended up living for a year and a half.

Houston is just a collage of memories. I had very little conception of time. I couldn't stop thinking about how things could've and would've been, but I wanted to get back in school before I was too old. Ronald was just a few years older than me. He helped register me but I had to fill in all the blanks.

My high school environment in Texas felt more like a junior college. Alicf Hastings was state-of-the-art compared to our old rundown buildings in New Orleans. The grass was cut extra short and students from all different cultures—Black, white, Asian, Hispanic—chilled under the shade of the trees.

I had to get up before the sun to catch the yellow bus, which I hadn't done since elementary. In New Orleans, we got bus tickets to ride public transit. On the first day, I met the administration who warned that any violence or disrespect from us newcomers would not be tolerated. All of the kids from New Orleans huddled up near the flower bed by the cafeteria door. At lunch, the girls from New Orleans would hold a dance contest in the middle of the courtyard to see who could shake the best. The Houston girls tried to imitate them but their rhythm was off. The guys usually walked to the football stadium adjacent to the school to smoke cigarettes and shoot dice.

Once all the New Orleans kids found out about the basketball court hidden on the backside of the school, endless truth or dare games went on. A gangbanger from Texas got slapped on the back of the neck because someone dared a N.O. kid to do it. The kid turned so red he could have started a fire. He told the assistant principal that a kid with dreads did it, which was impossible to distinguish because everyone from N.O. wore dreadlocks, even the girls used weaves to create the effect.

Chicks from Texas were fixed on hair when chasing a boyfriend. They would say, "I want to tread with the dreads." Which meant a New Orleans boy with dreadlocks. I guess our appearance got us girls and trouble. I got caught in the back of the gym smoking Kool menthols with my friend Leland and a Houston kid who wanted to be down with us. They gave me a Texas boot out of the school, and suggested an alternative school that my friends said was like prison. I didn't go back to school in Houston.

I was upset, but it wasn't as bad as my experience with the Houston police. Ronald, Sandals and I had an apartment in the southwest section of the city. One day after school, Ronald cooked chicken and macaroni and we were smoking while playing Madden. There was a knock. Ronald opened the door, saw a man with all black on, closed it in his face, and locked the door. We could hear him outside with a walkie-talkie. We didn't know what was going on—whether someone was trying to attack us or arrest us. We flushed the weed down the toilet and Ronald got his pistol and went out the window onto the balcony.

The next thing I knew, our apartment was surrounded by cops with Sandals barking in my room. I was scared. I turned off the lights and could see the lights flashing outside. The cops said, "I see your ass! You better open the door." They kicked in the door and came in fifty deep. They grabbed me, put me on the ground, and had their feet on my head. One said, 'I could blow your fucking face off." I said, "I'm a juvenile!"

"I don't give a damn!"

They brought in a K-9 German Shepherd and it scuffled with Sandals. The next thing I heard was "Boom!" It sounded like a shotgun. Sandals cried out, and the fighting stopped.

I saw the blood spot as they led me out in handcuffs. The K-9s found Ronald hiding in another New Orleanian's apartment. I had to spend the night in a detention center because I was underage and didn't have anyone to come pick me up. There was only one other dude in there for truancy and he was from New Orleans too. The next day my sister Ashley signed me out. Ronald was in jail for a week. When he found

From left: Kareem, his brother Steven, and Ronald, courtesy of Kareem Kennedy.

out Sandals had been killed, he couldn't believe it. We had made it out of the storm together and been like family.

Way afterwards, they told us they had gotten a call that a Mexican had been kidnapped in our complex, and they thought we were responsible. We had to fight to stay in the apartment, but we lost. Ronald and I moved around for a few months until we decided to come home.

Eleventh Grade

When I first came back to New Orleans, it looked like a skeleton and resources were scattered. I was walking through the dark shadows of post-Katrina alone with the goal of getting my life stabilized.

I had to register for school at an elementary school uptown. An administrator told me all the credits she had for me were from Kennedy. She needed Alief Hastings, my school in Texas, to fax a transcript to them in order for them to put me in the 11th grade. Hastings said I owed them for textbooks, and I had to pay two hundred dollars to clear the hold on my name. When they sent the transcript, I found out I only had a half a credit for each class because of my expulsion. I was looking at doing another dreaded year of high school.

There were four different schools to choose from: Robouin, Clark, Douglas, and John McDonogh. At the end of the summer, I received a letter in the mail saying that I was only eligible to go to the Mac. The school had been ridiculed as an underachieving and low performing school. The killing of a senior at John Mac in 2003 hardened the school's reputation for being terrible and it was taken over by the state.

After the first day, I knew it was going to be a long year. When I walked through the gate, I was overtaken with the feeling of being back in a school setting. At age 17 in the 11th grade, I felt the pressure

John McDonogh Senior High, by Kareem Kennedy.

to drop out or get fully focused on graduation.

On that first day, kids looked prepared to complete the school year. Everyone had their book sacks and their shirts tucked in. By the end of the day, the backpacks were lost and the shirts were hanging out of pants. After about a week, many kids just came to school with jokes on their mind and fresh shoes. Students folded tablets and shoved them into back pockets like it wasn't today's lesson.

Security proved to be more of a problem than a solution for control of the students. Some were too aggressive like the one guard who everyone called Blue Eyez. The poor guy took his job as seriously as a soldier in Iraq. He had Popeye's arms and walked around like a cowboy who was trying to stake his territory.

Before the storm, the schools, like the city, were divided by wards. The year the school opened after the storm, it was opened to students from across the whole city. People from the Seventh Ward and the St. Bernard identified themselves by skulls, skulls, skulls. Just looking around necks, on backpacks, drawn on notebooks and on hoodies, you would know a Hard Head was present. At school, people from the Seventh Ward usually chilled together. Every time someone from the Seventh passed, you could hear "Yoooo!" When the project was still functioning, that was a way to get a person's attention. One time, I was in a crowded RTA bus and before I could get off, yells of "Yooo!" came from down the block. I looked back and it was Mario flailing his arms across each other.

Hood art also became a problem for the school. I think the tagging of the St. Bernard Project (S.B.P) drawn with a red marker with the list of names under it was the catalyst. Before you could say beaucoup, the hallways were filled with literature like "Lil Red Luvs 6th Ward Bee" and not very good drawings of skulls. Even in books, you'd find a handwritten smack in the face. I remember one time in fifth period English, we had to read a passage out of the textbook. As I was awaiting my turn to read, I skimmed through the chapters until I noticed a handwritten note that said, "If you are looking @ dis u gay! Ha ha ha!"

That whole first year, I told myself I was in eleventh, when the system still said tenth. The school came up with the idea of the "recovery credits" when it became clear there were a lot of students in a similar position. A significant number of students were behind on their credits, but I was one of only ten that took advantage of the program. The school was a lot less intense without all the kids running, the teachers screaming, and the security patrolling the halls. After the regular day was over, I'd have a thirty minute break that I used to clear my mind and start again. It was lonely, but I was focused.

Jamal Robertson in his classroom, by Rachel Breunlin.

Interview with John Mac Social Studies Teacher, Jamal Robertson

John Mac had a few teachers who could actually display authority and teach at the same time. In most of my classes, the students would talk over the teacher, be disrespectful to others, and even gamble.

The first year at the Mac, my chemistry teacher, a young graduate from Harvard, tried her best. I didn't like chemistry, but the way she broke it down started to make sense. The students didn't care that she graduated from Harvard and said hurtful things. I defended her and would click out on the class, telling them, "Y'all fucking tripping, this lady could be teaching anywhere." I was so mad when I heard she had quit. I hope she's doing okay.

One of the only people in the school students didn't play with was Brother Rob. One of the coolest, most honest teachers who was actually respected by students. He is a history teacher on the second floor. The first time I saw him I knew he was for real. His bald head, black-rimmed glasses, and thick goatee made you think he was some type of revolutionary professor.

Brother Rob's approach to students is no B.S. He doesn't care if you're a girl or boy, tough or timid—if he caught you down bad he would have a talk with you. On the first day everyone was very talkative. Brother came to the front and said with power, "This is the Black." Everyone looked at each other in confusion, then he said, "That's what I call this room, 'The Black.'" Looking around he had a large painting of a Black man breaking chains, an oversized picture of a lion, and a portrait of Tupac that looks more like Brother Rob. I thought to myself, "This guy is going to challenge me."

When a lot of teachers didn't mind if you skipped a class for two lunches, Brother Rob would find you and get your parents involved. People's parents usually took Brother Rob's side even though their children accused him of wrongdoing.

At the start of every class he would give us a topic to talk about, ranging from personal perceptions to opinions on social issues. He told us we were African scholars and had high expectations for everyone. When the class got out of the way he would tell us stories about former students who were just like us. He would describe how they were acting in school, how much potential they had, but how the streets had broken them down—to scare us out of ignorant decisions.

Brother Rob's parents, Dwight Robertson and Lillian Conway, courtesy of Jamal Robertson.

Kareem: Where did you grow up?

Brother Rob: I grew up right on Republic Street in Gentilly.

Kareem: Can you describe the typical things that go on?

Brother Rob: When I was coming up?

Kareem: Yes.

Brother Rob: I lived in a fairly decent neighborhood, in my opinion. We had a neighborhood filled with children and we really played like children. We weren't forced to be adults. On the weekends, after we watched the cartoons, we played from sun up to sun down after we completed our chores. On weekdays, everybody was inside. After everybody did their homework, the whole neighborhood rushed outside.

Kareem: What did your parents do for a living?

Brother Rob: My father was the first Black machinist in this city so he made fairly decent money. As far as my mother, she worked raising us. That was her job. She put her career on the side to raise all of us. She didn't want us to go to nurseries and places like that. Once everybody graduated, my mother went back to school and got her degree. I got a degree before my mother did.

Kareem: What exactly is a machinist?

Brother Rob: Machinists are mathematicians. They can give you measurements and fractions. My father built things out of steel and metal. If you go out and see a large ship, he makes different products from the metals. He was an enforcer with the work. We had to do homework—that was important to him. I really had a daddy.

Kareem: How many siblings do you have?

Brother Rob: I have two brothers and two sisters.

Kareem: What high schools and colleges did you attend?

Brother Rob: I went to Warren Easton. I went to a school called Redeemer High and I went to Grambling State University.

Kareem: Is it any different now than when you went?

Brother Rob: It's a lot different. When I went to school, we weren't angels, but we still respected our elders and each other. A simple example: When I was in school, we would never open up a teacher's door to peep in or to look for another student. We didn't have the courage because we respected our elders too much. Today, it appears to me that our youth don't really respect adults—authority.

Some of our parents want to be our best friends. Some people think that's great, but I don't. I think you should be able to talk to your parents about anything, but it's got to be at a certain level. I can't talk to you like I'm your peer. I have students who are sixteen years old. On the street, they hang with people my age. They can't distinguish the difference because the adult is doing the same things the children are doing. The mamas want to dress like the daughters. The mothers talk about males to their daughters like they are speaking with adult friends.

Kareem: What was your favorite subject in school?

Brother Rob: It always changed and depended on the teacher. I had an English teacher who was so difficult and firm. We had seven classes. We had thick books and big book sacks and I took my time and did his homework. It took me an hour or two. Got to

school, left my homework in the locker. As soon as I walked in the classroom, I realized I forgot it and asked, "Can I go to my locker?" I hadn't sat down, but the man told me no. That taught me a lesson about being aware. Responsibility. I had a physics teacher who was the man. Sometimes it took a minute for us to grasp the concept, but because of his knowledge and ability to give us hands-on experiments, everybody loved his class.

Kareem: What was your major in college?

Brother Rob: Social science education. It entails psychology, sociology, American history, world history, geography, civics and free enterprise. Those are the courses that I can teach and have taught over the years at John McDonogh.

Kareem: How long have you been teaching?

Brother Rob: Since 1996. Before I taught, I worked offshore on an oil rig and I made good money. I was a young man, about 19 years old. But I didn't like it. To me, it was like prison. You caught a helicopter out there and nothing is around you but water. I couldn't swim. You share a room with five guys. I mean, I couldn't leave. I was out there for 14 days, then home, then back out again.

I left that and came to John McDonogh to work as a paraprofessional in 1992. At first, I only wanted it to make the money. I was the same age as the students' age. They had students older than me, but the principal, Raynard Sanders, really took a chance on me. He was like, "How are they gonna respect this boy?" Once I got into the system and saw the students and the teachers, I had love for it.

I became interested in educating. I didn't have a degree so I went to Grambling. It was the best decision I ever made—to leave home and deal with so many Black minds who were intelligent, who had a thirst for knowledge. It motivated me to want to learn, and even want to teach.

When you have a sense of self, you become anchored. You respect yourself and you love yourself. Then, and only then, can you respect and love other people. Once I know who I am, you can't tell me about me. When you know your roots, and have great people around you that look like you, it inspires you to say, "I can do that. I love that. I'm proud of that. I am that." It only brings out the best in you.

Kareem: Why do people call you Brother Rob?

Brother Rob's grandfather, Ernest Conway, courtesy of Jamal Robertson.

Brother Rob: I've been called a lot of things since I've been here. Somebody started calling me that. I mean, they called me Big Brother Rob, Brother Rob, Guerilla Rob—I have all types of names.

Kareem: Well, how long have you been called –

Brother Rob: Brother Rob? I've been here 12 years—maybe about eight of those 12. They had a program called Creole Cottage. It was a carpentry program, and the students actually went into the community and built houses. They made me a sign that said, "Brother Rob."

Kareem: How did you get interested in history?

Brother Rob: I always knew I was going to college but my dad didn't say, "Boy, you going to college." It's just the conversations and the things we talked about. I always had an interest in my personal family history and then it grew from there.

My grandfather was a construction worker and he worked with the union. He really fought for Black folk who didn't know their rights—the Black folk who were getting shortchanged. He knew how to read, and even though his job and his life were at jeopardy, he still stood up for those people. He was well-respected by the people who could not read, or just didn't have the gumption, the heart, or the know-how.

It was powerful. When you see him, you can actually visualize it. That's so important—anything you can really see, you can do it. When I saw my grandfather, I could see me: "I would like to do that. I would like to be respected like my grandfather."

Kareem: Who are your favorite historians to teach the students?

Brother Rob: I like a man named John Henrik Clark. As a boy, he had to drop out of elementary school to help support his family. As a scholar, he was self-taught, although later he earned a Masters and a PhD. He read everything. When he went to school, it was a one-room school and you had people from different grade levels together. When he finally was on the university level, he knew more than his professors. His professors allowed him to teach classes because Clark was more knowledgeable than his degreed instructors. His degree was waiting for him in the dean's office whenever he was ready. He's before Malcolm X and Martin Luther King. He's a true historian and helped create African American Studies.

Kareem: Were you at the school when the shooting took place?

Brother Rob: Yes.

Kareem: What impact did it have on you? What happened from your perspective?

Brother Rob: It was something that carried over from the neighborhood. And when violence carries over from the neighborhood, that happens because—plain and simple—we don't know our history. Knowing your history really changes everything. When these children come to my class and they learn their history, it not only changes their behavior in the school, but out in the community. Once they learn something, they can't help but to teach it. If not verbally then just by living it.

When I went to the gym that morning to look for somebody, I had a feeling that I couldn't explain. I couldn't find him, so I left. As soon as I got into the main

Display of Martin Luther King and Malcom X in Brother Rob's classroom, by Rachel Breunlin.

building, I heard the shooting. The way it impacted me? It just lets me know that we're lacking something somewhere. We're missing something and what we're missing, for the most part, is parenting skills. Since we don't have parents, youngsters are out on the street with no responsibility, with no discipline. They can make their own decisions and they're not equipped to make certain decisions. You have children who are acting on impulses. You have a child just trying to survive out here in the world. When somebody does something to them, their mind is not developed enough. Their emotions are not developed enough to handle the situation properly.

Kareem: How many students over the years have you lost to violence?

Brother Rob: I don't know, Kareem. Every year I lose more than one student. About seven years ago, I stopped going to funerals because it was too much for me. I went to a funeral every year and to see the youngster in a coffin and the parents and the family and the friends—how they broke down, how emotional they were—I just couldn't deal with it. It was wearing at me. To maintain my strength, I had to stop. I don't go. No disrespect to the families, but it wasn't good for me personally.

Kareem: How does John Mac remember students who are killed?

Brother Rob: I don't think they do. I don't think the school as a whole, as an institution, does. Individuals might do certain things but school-wide, they don't.

Kareem: What do you think about the memorial shirts as history?

Brother Rob: I have mixed thoughts on that. I think you want to remember, but I think you have to sometimes let go and appreciate. I'm not saying forget, though, because that is history and make no mistake, you always remember and acknowledge your ancestors—that's who they are, that's who they become. They're your people, your family, your friends. You don't want to lose that.

Everybody has different opinions. I think you never die. That's my opinion and I mean that literally not just because you are living on in my mind. Your body, your physical form, may die but your essence still exists. Maybe it's just consciousness or awareness and it becomes part of a bigger consciousness.

Kareem: Don't you think sometimes it creates beef?

Brother Rob: I think it can and it does. For example, if you go back to the shooting up in the school, there were people who knew the shooter and the person who was shot. Those shirts have the potential to initiate some form of hostility and/or action.

Now, if you gave me that shirt, I would take it and hold it, but I wouldn't wear that in public. And no disrespect to the person. I watch cars today and they have "R.I.P." with a person's name on it. I think that's ignorance. This is not a public thing. It's like I'm showing off—like I need you to know what I'm doing. You're advertising.

All these "RIPs" should change to "LIPs" (Live in Peace). When we have family, and we have love and history, RIP should be gone. We can do away with that.

Kareem: What reaction do you get when you tell people that you teach at John Mac?

Brother Rob: I think I often get a negative reaction. I rarely tell people I'm a teacher, like talking about it. That's not something I come up and say unless somebody's inquisitive and they ask. But I got a negative response, like, "Oh you teach over there," or they may even look at me funny, like maybe I am not a true teacher, or I teach there because I can't teach anywhere else. Others give me the utmost respect because they understand the daily challenges.

I was at McDonogh 35 after the storm, and we had students and teachers from different schools all over the city. The students from 35 had an arrogance and were upset because all of these intruders: "This is our school." I can understand that coming from a young mind, but at the same time the city had been through a crisis.

The original teachers at 35 looked down at the other children and teachers who came from different schools as well. Now here's my point. If you're at McDonogh 35, you have a certain caliber of student. From elementary, these children already have a certain knowledge base, and exposure to discipline. You give them the work and they automatically know certain things. You come up in John McDonogh— this child reads on a third grade level, this child reads on a sixth grade level. You really have to break things down. You really have to teach!

The teachers at 35 couldn't handle the new students. They had to literally put their pride aside and turn to the teachers from the other schools. Instead of sitting back and being humble and respectful and saying, "Wow, I'm at 35 and I love my children, but our eyes have been opened," they looked down at the other teachers. It's sad because as a teacher, you always are learning. You always have to pay attention to your students because they give clues, which allows the teacher to understand the best strategies and styles to communicate lessons. If you listen to the students, they can show you how to deliver this history, this biology.

Kareem: Yeah, it's different. To me, each school has its own culture.

Brother Rob: Right, every school has its own climate and environment—atmosphere—because every area in this city is different. Uptown is different from downtown. The Ninth Ward and the Lower Ninth Ward are different. New Orleans East is different from Gentilly. It's so great to bring the schools together because that cuts down on the foolishness. Bring the schools together and let them collaborate and work together. When I was in high school, if you had been at Fortier, you might fight Carver, but if you're from Fortier and I'm from Carver and we were working on this debate team together, I can say, "Oh that's my boy, Kareem," and eliminate that right there.

Kareem: Why did you choose to stay at John Mac all these years?

Brother Rob: Because the people here are me. I wanted to come back because I think it's a greater need over here. I think it's easier at 35, but I just want to be here. Let me tell you, I had been teaching about three years. After three years you're tenured. I had a friend who taught at Warren Easton. Now mind you, I attended Warren Easton. He said, "Man, give me your resume. I got a connection and I got this and I got that." Mind you, it's a wonderful and proud feeling to teach where you learned. Where you sat in this class and walked these halls. I said, "No, I can't do it. If all the good teachers go to Warren Easton, who's going to be at John Mac?" He couldn't believe I said that. I mean, he really got quiet for a while trying to figure out why in the world would I want to turn an offer down like that.

Kareem: Yeah, how do you manage to control your class in an orderly fashion?

Brother Rob: I set rules and I expect the students to follow them. But I think I really respect myself and I respect the students—that's why they follow the rules. I can't make you do anything. Students choose to do what's right.

I think we want structure, Kareem. I think these students who walk around like they don't know better, *do* know better and they want you to lay the foundation. They want you to hold their feet to the fire, and when you do, you're really letting them know that you care about them. Students appreciate that. Human beings appreciate that. Now they're going to complain, they're going to resist, but deep down they know what's going on. They feel it. Sometimes even though they know what's right they still have to work on it because we have so many bad habits: "I want to do right, but dang!" They take a minute and I don't expect things overnight. You learn patience.

I have coworkers who come from all of these top-notch schools and they wouldn't dare to send their child to this school. They brag about, "My child goes to this school and that school." So you already know what it takes. You come from it and you let these children do anything they want? "You can play cards in the class? You can come late? You can have your headphones on? Mr. Smith cool." Mr. Smith's really not cool. Mr. Smith is really not concerned with you.

I don't really like to sit in a classroom and students just doing what they want. I don't feel comfortable. I feel like a thief, like a cheat. Growing up, I played ball throughout New Orleans so the whole city's really my playground. I don't really just claim I'm Gentilly. Everything is mine. Everything is there for me and the more you travel the more you feel like that. Go to New York, go to Jamaica, go to Paris, go to Zimbabwe and watch how you stop talking about the Sixth Ward. That's small minded. You're talking about the Sixth Ward. Man, I'm coming back from Russia. I still have snow in my boots. Everybody doesn't do things the way you do things. They don't talk the same, the food is different.

Kareem: Do you plan on changing positions such as principal or another?

Brother Rob: No, that's not my thing. I think you know your niche. I mean, maybe later, but right now I'm not that type of soldier. The classroom's my thing. I like the students. That's where my relationship is, that's where my heart is.

Kareem: What message do you try to pass along to students?

Brother Rob: To always do your best.

Kareem: Have you made gains in doing so?

that's weakness leaving your body. You're getting stronger. I don't care if I'm lifting weights, or I'm trying to read this and write that—all of this struggle leads to improvement.

Kareem: What do you think schools need to provide for boys and girls to succeed?

Brother Rob: In our communities, we need to learn more about entrepreneurship, self-employment. We need to learn how to sustain ourselves and our families. We need to have someone in our classrooms teaching us about economics. Right now, the system's set up to learn how to work for other people. We learn how to be followers. If I were to start a school on an elementary level, we would start businesses in our class—selling apples, t-shirts, making things. For the most part, anybody who starts their own business—even if they lose the business—doesn't want to work for anybody again. You really become self-actualized because everything depends on you.

Kareem: What about the way the school looks, do you think that impacts how kids go to school?

Brother Rob: I have, you know, and I say you always do your best because everybody doesn't learn at the same rate. Everybody don't start out on the same level. "I can't do what you do, Kareem, but I know if I work hard I can do this and I can do that." I'm not going to make excuses. We complain about everything. Stop complaining and start training.

Let me tell you a lesson I learned, Kareem. One of the best things I ever did at John McDonogh was getting to coach the girls' softball team. I laid down discipline, giving them short-term goals, reaching them, and then accomplishing the long-term goal. When you're going through that pain or suffering,

Brother Rob: No, it's irrelevant to a degree. You can tell an old man, 60 years old, how raggedy the building was and he'll tell you the building they had was falling apart—no heat, cold—but they learned and they learned because they wanted it. I can put you in any building, and if you want it, you're going to get it. When we came up, we didn't even have a rim on the basketball goal. We took matches and burned out the bottom of a crate and hung it up. No backboard so you really had to master that shot. That's how we shot basketball and all those boys who went on to play in high school started because they wanted it.

Kareem: What was your concept of me when you saw me for the first time, when you got to know me?

Brother Rob: I can't answer that objectively because when I first met you I was already biased because I knew your brother, Steven. I already had a concept of who you were based on the respect that you had for your brother. When I met you at the House of Blues, Steven said, "That's my brother," and you were looking up at your brother like he's the greatest, you know? If your brother is doing well, I know where your head is, where you're trying to go based on him.

And then I met you at a poetry reading, if I'm not mistaken. That's something right there. And you're riding your bike to work. That's something. I've heard kids say, "I'm not riding no bike. I'm not catching no bus to work." Why you didn't go to work? "I ain't had no ride." But you meeting your brother at the poetry session just getting off from work—that had a little bit of power in that for me.

LARRY "LIL LARRY" RAMEE III

RAMEE Larry "Lil Larry' Ramee III, on Saturday, March 24, 2007 went home to receive his mansion, robe and crown. "Lil Larry' was born on July 1, 1990 to his caring parents Larry Ramee, Jr. and Selika "Leeky' Thomas. Stepson of Keshana Ramee and Erroll O. Thomas, Jr. and his father's companion Nicole Gatlin. Loving grandson and stepson of Kathy Alexander and Larry Ramee, Sr., Bernard and Marilyn Sanchez. He leaves to cherish his memories, siblings: Lance and Kimiani Ramee, Erroll J. Thomas III, Lyric Steel and Lloyd and Ja'Bria Turner. Loving aunt and uncles Danetta and Reneda Ramee, Santrice Ducro, Janelle Johnson, Derrick Turner, Bernard and Daniel Sanchez. Great grandson of Janetta "Mrs. Polou' Alexander. Also survived by devoted friend Cherelle Hall; god parents Ronald Williams and Tanika Carter, a host of relatives, cousins and friends. Preceded in death by his great grandfather Willie Alexander. Relatives, friends, employees, faculties, students and staffs of Save-A-Center, Frederick Douglas and John McDonogh High Schools are invited to attend the funeral. A Service will be held on Saturday, March 31, 2007 at CHARBONNET-LABAT FUNERAL HOME, 1615 ST. PHILIP STREET at 1:00 PM. Interment Mt. Olivette Cemetery. Visitation 12 noon in the FAMILY CENTER. CHARBONNET-LABAT, Directors 581-4411

Published in The Times-Picayune on 3/30/2007.
Notice • Guest Book • Flowers • Gift Shop • Charities

Today's The Times-Picayune death notices

Twelfth Grade

Short, stout, and a head full of natty locks stood my ace Larry. When you ask around about the life of Larry, all you will hear are positive things. I first met him when I tried out for park ball at Willie Hall Park. I didn't get a chance to play an actual game because I never took a physical but I went to practice because it was something to do. Larry's dad always pushed him harder than other kids. Long after park ball practices were over, Larry would have to please his father by running sprints. After a bad performance in a game, he scolded him. His dad always showered him with gifts when Larry had done good in school or on the field.

As park-ballers, we had a tight bond that would not be broken over the years. On other days, I would be posted on the sidewalk, just outside the courtway, chillin with the hood and before you saw Larry you would hear Lil Gerald and Lil Lance, Larry's brothers, zoom pass on mini bikes (Baby Harley's Pocket Rockets) going up Gibson and then returning in front of us like the Matrix. He would give dap on the corner and sometimes, if you asked him, he'd let you push the minibike.

Larry was the coolest dude you could ever meet because he always was himself. At Gregory Junior High, where I attended two years of school, I learned from Lae. He taught me the importance of being responsible and humble. Fighting? Not Lae. Smoking? Not Lae. Stealing? Not Lae. Deceit? Not Lae. He traveled the path of the righteous. Easy to be friends with, hard not to love him.

When Larry returned to New Orleans after the storm, his family moved to a house on Broad Street. The first time we ran into each other was at the Exclusive Barbershop, which is run by Kev and Rody—two well-known barbers in our area. We greeted each other with a ghetto handshake and talked for a while, reminiscing about our old Gregory days.

We were at different schools now. Larry was in the 11th at Douglas Senior High School in the Ninth Ward. On school mornings, I would be on my way walking towards the Mac, and Lae would be standing at the Broad and St. Bernard bus stop where he awaited the school bus destined for Doug. We would holla at each other about school life and he'd say, "Look at Reem—smart as cheese, *and* you smoke." I would crack a smile because his words made me proud to be me. One time, I was walking to school up Broad Street with my dog Joe when Lae pulled on

the side of us with his younger brother Lance. He had his license and he got to drive his people's car every now and then. He offered us a ride, we accepted, and got in the back. He was bumping Young Gunz's "Never take Me Alive."

After a few semesters, I saw Lae and his aunt in the front office at the Mac, which surprised me. He said he would be transferring from Doug to the Mac because it was closer and more convenient for him. I was excited because someone I knew from the hood would help pass time with me—you know, like old times.

We didn't have any classes together, but we would meet on the steps that led up to the auditorium mostly with friends from the projects and the Seventh Ward, socializing about rappers, sports, and females we were aiming to get at. After school, I'd catch Larry walking with close friends from Orchid's Seafood or Tastee's, the donut shop.

In the Spring of 2007, when the city reopened the St. Bernard Project to be cleaned and gutted out, Larry volunteered his time to help. And when people from the Housing Development found out the city was trying to shut down the project for good, community activists sponsored protests to stop demolition and all of us took part in them. In March, we talked about how happy we would be to pass the LEAP test. Graduation was what Larry wanted most.

On March 25, I did my routine of watching the news at 10 p.m. to see what was happening around the city. The news report told the story of a sixteen-year-old boy who was shot and killed in a drive-by at the stoplight at Broad and Orleans. They also said that he wrecked trying to escape the spray of bullets. One male and two passengers survived. It showed a dark colored car showered with bullets. I thought to myself, "That's messed up."

The next day came. When I was headed to the gas station, I saw my uncle Abbie walking towards me. He said, "That's cold blooded what they did to your friend." I said, "What friend?"

"You didn't hear? Lil Larry was killed last night."

Immediately my head was spinning out of control. I walked away from my uncle and headed for the barbershop. I couldn't believe him. I asked my barber if it was true and he confirmed what my uncle had told me. My eyes cried a river. I was enraged, ready to explode. I walked back to the trailer and just sat there for hours. After awhile, my friends and family started calling me, grieving and letting me know that Tahara, Wallisha, Jessica, and Delly all survived. Wallisha was in the hospital in critical condition.

I missed a few days of school to cool off because I felt like I would snap on someone if they looked at me wrong. Larry was buried a week after the tragedy. On that Saturday morning of the funeral, thoughts of "This can't be life," raced through my head: How can a person who embodies GOD, righteousness, truth, be laid down in a box? Mario and I met up to view Larry's body one last time. On our way there, we found out he was killed because of mistaken identity. The shooters had just aimed through tinted windows and fired.

The funeral was mega packed—wall-to-wall people gathered to say good-byes. I stood behind a few young girls who wore "In memory of" t-shirts with Larry's picture on them. As the preachers started the ceremonies people began to weep and pass out. I saw Larry's dad, Big Larry. He looked as if he took it the hardest. I couldn't see Larry from my view. I still couldn't believe it.

Preachers, teachers, and family spoke good things about him. A man who knew Larry said he often asked him to sing "A Change is Gonna Come" by Sam Cooke. He began singing the song. I felt his soul and began to cry.

At the end of the funeral, the preacher told everyone to form a line to view Larry for the last time. As people went one by one, many glanced at Lae and burst into tears. Some of my friends didn't cry. I guess many of them had already been too familiar with death and just shook it off quickly. As for myself, I had a real tough time. Larry's wake was the first I ever attended. As the funeral went on, I began to feel a sudden voltage through my veins. Not like a shock, but a stimulating rush through my body. I looked at

Larry closely and said a prayer in my mind. It made me mad when I thought of living and breathing life.

I exited the funeral home. I saw everyone who was already outside mourning, in pain. I saw Lance. I hardened up and told him, "It gone be all right. He's watching over us."

After they put Larry in the ground, the rest of the day honored Larry at places that were important to him—his family's house, the St. Bernard Center where he loved to go swimming, and a teenage club where he partied on the weekends. The repass at the gym of the center was packed wall to wall. A DJ played music—all the sounds us teenagers like to hear. His family supplied beaucoup food and cold drinks. I grabbed a plate of crawfish and a Sprite, and sat outside on the hood of one of the parked cars. Friends gathered and we talked about the situation while smoking exotic herbs and drinking daiquiris. The music and crowd rocked for hours. The police and military police rolled by a few times. Near the end, a second line band arrived and tore it down. Everybody broke out their footwork one last time for Larry.

Later that night, his family threw a party for him at Club Escape, a hole in the wall, which seemed to be named for its patrons' efforts to escape the building because of a rowdy fight or gunfire. The blueprint is simple: a bar, dance-stage, and pool table—one way in, and one way out. Instead of risking more drama, I decided to go home, smoke some more herbs, and rest.

As days passed, I thought about the funeral and all the people who cared and loved him. The people he touched. He is one of the reasons I wake up with ambition and GOD on my mind—any day can be your last. I feel Lae when the winds blow, and when the sun rises. I ask him, in my prayers, to watch my back when I'm on these cold streets. From time to time, my friends and I talk about Lae. When I think of him, he taught me that true friends are hard to find and they never die. They are a part of you.

JOHN MCDONOGH SENIOR HIGH SCHOOL

COMMENCEMENT EXERCISE

MCDONOGH NO. 35   SENIOR HIGH SCHOOL
AUDITORIUM

1331 KERLEREC STREET
NEW ORLEANS, LA

FRIDAY, JUNE 6, 2008
10:00 AM

The Top Ten

Miriam Karina Contreras
Hazzarra Dykes
Oscar Joseph Williams
Angela S. Payne
Ariel Lindell Scipio

Ronnie Thomas
Kierra Marie Battee
Evangeline Hills
Tiara Ariane Newsome
Sharday Miner

Joseph Adams
Lamar Allen
Kevin Ard
Jasper August
Kiera Battee
Phillip Belcher
Andrea Bell
Cedric Bishop
Kourtney Bolds
Waneisha Boutte
Dedrese Branch
Ahmad Braud
Erica Brooks
Bruce Brown
Steven Brown
Tyler Brumfield
Terrance Burton
Arielle Buxton
Mario Cannon
Harrison Carter
Harry Carter
Feltus Clark
Orian Condall
Miriam Contreras
Angie Crawford
Takia Crayton
Kenneth Dalcour
Ashley Davis
Jomonique Dorsey
Hazzarra Dykes
Jovell Edwards
Urra Feltus
Toya Gray
Ashanti Foley
Jessica Francis
Joshua Francois

Michelle Freeman
Garineka Hall
April Hampton
Darnell Harris
Eliska Harrison
Shawn Hartford
Amanda Hatch
Melvin Henderson
Keith Hill
Reginald Hilliard
Evangeline Hills
Jasmine Hollinger
Vernon James
Aramis Jasmine
Aaron Johnson
Adrian Johnson
Janice Johnson
Arrington Jones
Brittnay Joseph
Chelsea Keller
Kareem Kennedy
Jerome Lewis
Trinice Mackey
Tahira Marigny
Christa Marshall
Kirt Martin
D'Arianne Maxson
Johnnie McLeod
Dwight Miner
Sharday Miner
Jonathan Montrel
Hakeena Nelson
Tiara Newsome
Chad Nicholas
Stacey Olidge
Justina Panes
Zyekita Parker

Angela Payne
Christian Porter
Denise Preston
Mikell Preston
Kennette Price
Teara Ridgley
Lakeshia Rothchild
Nathlean Sartin
Ariel Scipio
Carey Seals
Corey Shaw
Earl Sipp
Danielle Smith
Dirrick Sorina
Arshaun Stevenson
Jenese Stewart
Joandea Summers
Calvin Tate
Cornisha Tate
Gregory Thomas
Kendrick Thomas
Ronnie Thomas
Winter Thomas
Adia Thompson
Rhonda Thompson
Angel Ward
Jairus Warren
Adam Washington
Ke'Visha Washington
Sade West
Janay Wheeler
Feliciana Williams
Oscar Williams
Christina Young
India Young
Rogers Youngblood

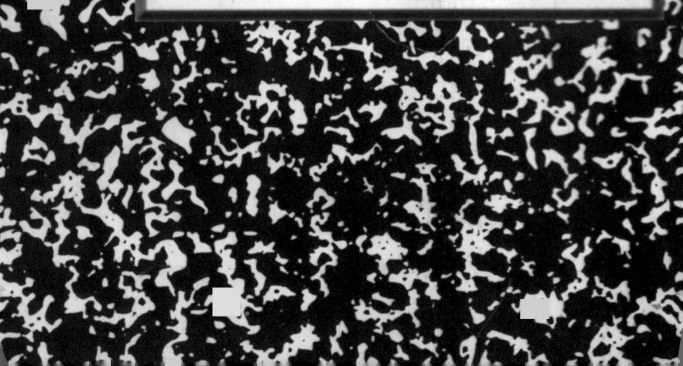

THE ORIGINAL

MARBLE COVER-48 SHEETS

NAME _Reen 3_

WIDE RULED
ROARING SPRING, PA 16673

College

Man ever since I graduated ^from school life
has come speeding at me. I thought
going to school and working was hard
when I was in. The day after graduation
I knew I had to do something
to keep me driven and have goals. I
filled out ^applications for a couple jobs for weeks
to no avail. The college applications I had
filled out at the end of the school
year had been thrown out of ^my mind be
cause of my academic background.

The College World

Soon after I graduated from the Mac, I knew things would take a drastic change. I had focused on graduating that whole school year, but now it was no more school worries. I had to deal with the real world.

I worked at several French Quarter joints. It was good money, but I needed to experience an environment that invited growth. When I entered the doors of local universities, I got a taste of higher education. It was amazing to see various cultures bustling around in one placc. I knew college would give me a chance to learn from my peers. My ACT scores weren't all that impressive. Still, I filled out applications to a few of the big names and received no responses. I decided to register for Delgado Community College. I figured it was a start, and the rest of the summer I spent running back and forth to Delgado to get paperwork done. Most of the time, I caught the bus, sometimes waiting hours for the RTA to come.

After the paperwork was over, I had idle time on my hands. I started filling out applications in the French Quarter with no luck except for a position at a hotel that was open two months down the line. I finally got a break when I asked the owner of a car wash not too far from where I was staying. He happened to be the father of a girl I went to school with. He taught me his routine for cleaning the vehicles and that was that. It wasn't the most professional of workplaces, but the money I made helped me get by until the summer was over. I would find myself in conversation with the customers, who ranged from musicians, policemen, friends, and the average Joe. I'd tell them, "I'm going to school," and they praised me and encouraged me, "You can do it."

When school started that semester, I began to grow nervous about Delgado. Coming from John Mac, I figured I was at a disadvantage in the college world. But my assumptions proved to be wrong when I started class and saw that my ideas and perceptions were respected by teachers. In psychology, I was taught by Dr. Gamble, who was very down to earth. He was portly, semi-bald, with a full, grey and white beard, and glasses. In his class, we learned about general psychology and psychological disorders—stages of sleep, neural transmitters, about emotion. His lectures put labels onto things I already knew. Because we talked about stuff that everybody could relate to, it was really interactive, engaging. I was the only Black boy in that class, which felt kind of weird, but Dr. Gamble made me feel comfortable enough to talk. I think he was from the Midwest, and the way he talked was slow but not boring. He would emphasize important things, and always asked for our input.

The professor told us his story, and it was a lot like mine. His parents were alcoholics. Growing up was rough with their drinking problems. I started to think about how drug addiction had become a cycle of abuse in my family and how I could break that cycle. I already had some help. My cousin John, who I had lived with in high school, was paying the rent at an apartment in the Bywater in an attempt to get me out of the hood.

I was juggling college and writing this book when another opportunity knocked on my door. Abram, my writing coach, told me if I signed up for Literacy AmeriCorps my site could be with the Neighborhood Story Project. I would work with him teaching children how to analyze literature and write poems. I thought, "How am I gonna teach someone who's only a few years younger than me?" My younger cousins always disobeyed me when I asked them to do something. How are they going to listen?

Delgado Community College, by Kareem Kennedy.

2008-2009 Literacy AmeriCorps, courtesy of Sarah Fischer.

Unconditional, Positive Regard

I was in a group of 17 strangers. Old and young, white and black, gay and straight, we came together to do AmeriCorps training, community service, and unity events like retreats to Mississippi. It felt weird being around a different mixture of people after so many years hanging with people from my hood, but since we all were working for AmeriCorps, I started to get more comfortable. Somebody I never would have talked to on the street, Adrian—an older white guy—told me stories about the Civil War and Creoles in downtown New Orleans. I got cool with the two dudes, B.J. and Nick—a black guy and white guy who were roommates—and would hang out at their house Uptown.

In the fall, we went to a Haunted History tour down in the French Quarter, and I was walking with Miriam and Molly. Miriam was studying sociology at Loyola—which was also my main interest in college. She was reserved and wasn't interested in materialism. I thought she was the opposite of a stereotypical snotty, white girl. She liked to mix the Bob Marley with the Jay-Z and the Alicia Keys, which I thought was cool. A lady leaned out of a jeep, and screamed at us, "Why are you with that nigger?!"

Miriam looked shocked, and I had a mean mug on my face. The moment brought me back in time to the old black/white days. I wanted to lash out at the woman, but the car was moving too fast. Molly and

From left: Molley Losey, Kareem, Miriam McGinn, and Adrian McGrath, courtesy of Sarah Fischer.

Miriam said, "People are so fucking stupid," and both hugged me.

A couple of weeks later, Miriam called me and invited me to come out with her and a group of AmeriCorps people. She said they were going to Frenchman Street to listen to some old timey jazz and blues at the Spotted Cat. I'd never hung out on Frenchman before because I always thought it was full of weirdos and never liked bars except when I needed a spot to watch the Saints' game.

But I liked Miriam and said, "I'll meet you there." We hung out for a few hours and then we went back to her house. She came behind me and started massaging my back. I was nervous. She was older than me, and I didn't know if I was going to make the right moves, but from that night on, we started dating.

A year before, I had a sweetheart who I thought was everything, but it turned out she wasn't ready for all that. I wasn't interested in a casual relationship. I felt like I was becoming a man and wanted unconditional, positive regard (aka love). Being with Miriam made my pride higher. My family and friends sometimes said, "What you doing with that white girl?" And I would say, "Her name is Miriam, and I love her." She was independent, living down here alone without family. She had a cat named Marley that she rescued from a shelter who was jealous of me. Every time I came around, he tried to scratch me. She was rational and sometimes didn't get my more poetic side, but I loved our discussions about language, politics, and just daily life. And I liked how, more and more, our lives were woven together. Once I told her, "I love you." She had to think about her response. That's how rational she was.

New Orleans Picayune

THURSDAY, JUNE 25, 2009

TELLING THEIR STORIES

to hold
iotic
c fest

usic festival
dependence Day
unday from 3 to
Episcopal
ckson Ave. The
bout 10 years
ted by **Albinas**
's director of
, who said he
e community of
an alternative
th of July Inde-
stivities."

red thoughts
for this year's

when I came
galow cottage, I
her visited me,"
The light blew
lamp as I en-
. I sensed my
ce. He was a
t killed in action
58."

edicating the
ther.

ell on the fact
y goes by with-
of this all-en-
edy in my life,"
But we move on
later."

n honor of all
, including **Bryan**
the Trinity
lied last March.
ll to know they
reciated," Priz-
country's

PHOTOS BY SCOTT McCROSSEN / FIVE65 DE

LEFT: Abram Himelstein, co-director of the Neighborhood Story Project in a classroom at Capdau. ABOVE: Andre Per CEO of the Capital One-UNO Charter School Network, looks over the shoulder of Capdau eighth-grader Shirley Cochran

Capdau eighth-graders are proud of new bool

Themes include sports, homework

By Joseph Halm
Contributing writer

Devin Jones enjoys sleeping so much that his mother calls him "Lazy Bones." But rather than take the nickname lying down, the young scribe used it as inspiration for "In that We Wrote So Much & Came So Far," a book penned by about 60 eighth-graders at Pierre A. Capdau Charter School for the Neighborhood Story Project.

Jones wrote his piece about a conversation he had with his bed, a discussion that ended with the bed encouraging him to become more active.

"It was basically a real-life thing," Jones said.

"Sometimes my mom calls me lazy because I like to sleep

Eighth-grader Jasmine Johnson is flanked by language arts teacher Kelly Rauser, left, and Kareem Kennedy, co-director of the

During the days in my AmeriCorps position, I was teaching poetry and creative writing to eighth graders in Ms. Rauser's class at Capdeau with Abram. At the end of the year, we were going to publish a book of their writing. Some days, it seemed like we were helping to shape their futures in a positive way. Other days got away from us and left me worrying that I had problems being an authority figure.

When they pushed Abram and me too far one day, I decided to give them a piece of tough love, and began preaching the virtues of education. I sounded like a cross between Marcus Garvey and Aunt Alice. I told them, "What we are teaching you are the skills you need to express yourself. Y'all are always talking about how your voices are not heard, here is your chance to make your voices heard, as Black youth." Everybody got quiet and started doing their work. I felt like a grown person talking to them like that. It seemed like just a few years ago I was getting told the same thing.

I asked Abram if we could teach some Langston Hughes and recycled the lessons of Mr. Reilhmann, my sixth grade teacher. We taught "Mother to Son" and "The Negro Speaks of Rivers" and their poems started to come alive. The class titled the book, *In That We Wrote So Much and Came So Far*, and we had a book release party that was covered on TV and in the newspaper.

My life was feeling solid. I was working on my book everyday, as a teacher two times a week, the hotel on the weekends, and going to Delgado. After a few months, I was usually staying over at Miriam's near Bayou St. John at night. We would hang out, walk by the bayou, or cook together. She had mindful food like quinoa. I cooked breakfast—grits, pancakes, sausage and eggs. One time, I went crabbing with Abram and we boiled crabs with Zatarain's and lemon. In my mind, I thought that I was doing the things a man should be doing—working, studying, having a relationship with a nice woman. Sometimes it seemed too good to be true.

Interview with Literacy AmeriCorps Coordinator, Sarah Fischer

I wanted to interview Sarah because she was the supervisor of Literacy AmeriCorps. We had built a solid, professional relationship. It had been my first time working at an organization that wasn't about earning money, but instead about developing character—mine and the people with whom I worked. I didn't feel like a machine at the job, but more like a person who actually had to use my intellect.

In the middle of the year, my responsibilities began to overwhelm me. School, writing the book, working at the hotel, and teaching poetry. I began to fumble away important pieces—frustrating those who depended on me. Sarah's leadership really came through. She helped me reset and work on my time management.

Sarah Fischer, by Lindsey Darnell.

Kareem: Hey Sarah, where are you from and where did you grow up?

Sarah: I was born in Florida, but I moved here when I was four. I grew up in Old Metairie, but I claim New Orleans proper as my home more than Old Metairie. I went to college in New York and spent about ten years in the northeast before coming back here.

Kareem: Wow. What was your school experience like?

Sarah: My parents taught at my high school, Metairie Park Country Day. My dad taught sex education to me in fifth grade so that was horrible. But it was fine after that. He was the disciplinarian, too,

and because he was an administrator, we lived in a house that was about a foot and a half from the edge of the French building. I knew all my teachers. They were all my parents' friends. It was cool to see them as family friends, versus just teachers. Then I went to Hamilton College in upstate New York and slacked off a little, which I regret. I'm in graduate school at Dartmouth now and hopefully I'll finish after I write my thesis.

Kareem: Where is Dartmouth?

Sarah: Hanover, New Hampshire, which is in the middle of nowhere New Hampshire. Well, most of New Hampshire is the middle of nowhere.

Kareem: How and why did you get involved in literacy?

Sarah: After 9/11, there were no jobs really in non-profit management in New York and teaching was kind of the easy way out and I really liked it. I taught for about five years and then when my husband came to Loyola Law School, I was interviewing for any jobs possible and randomly saw the ad on Craigslist for AmeriCorps. I didn't think I was gonna want to do it, but I was like, "I'll just interview." I really liked Rachel and liked what the job had to offer. Now it seems like the perfect fit to combine a lot of what I want to do. I'm hooked.

Kareem: What do you think about AmeriCorps as a kind of public education?

Sarah: I think the AmeriCorps system has a lot of potential. There's a lot of talk under the Obama Administration about everyone doing at least a year or two of service. George Bush II said that as well. I like that idea as a way to teach about civic engagement and giving back to your community. Some may disagree. The feedback I get from members is the year of service really helped them figure out what they wanted to do or helped kind of bridge a transition in their life.

Kareem: How do you think segregation in the school system impacted the city?

Sarah: I definitely think it's still impacting the city. You can see that. The school I went to was private and basically 100% white. Everyone's obsessed with black and white, but there's many different levels of that. I really feel like it's more of a Caribbean city where there's not just major segregation as far as race but also segregation as far as class—who are the acceptable black people to be in certain schools, who are the acceptable white people to be in certain schools.

Kareem: Had you been around people from such a diverse background before you took this job?

Sarah: I would love to say yes, but no, not really. I don't think I was as open to as many circles. When I left high school, I never wanted to come back to New Orleans. I was very jaded. I went to a very good private school and felt like I was poor because I was the faculty kid and didn't have the car and never would unless I bought it myself. Coming back to the city—both through this job and just the environment post-Katrina where everyone's had to help each other—I've really had an opportunity to meet people from diverse backgrounds. Not superficially diverse, and not just people who physically look different from me, but people who look exactly the same as me but have a completely different experience.

I think I've grown and hopefully I've been able to let other people grow. AmeriCorps is really diverse and it's been remarked on by other people how diverse our corps specifically has been, and that's awesome for me.

Kareem: What is it like working with people from different class and racial backgrounds, people from different places and age groups?

Sarah: I think it's hard in a way, especially because a lot of my job is planning trainings. Some of those trainings required by AmeriCorps were not so successful. We did an anti-racism workshop—and I think there was not enough follow-up.

Kareem: It was confusing and they didn't give enough strategies on how to combat actual situations.

Sarah: Yeah, that's what a lot of the members said. It's an interesting discussion to examine the history of

From left: Kareem, Kenneth Bryan, Adrian McGrath and Molley Losey, courtesy of Sarah Fischer.

race and create a uniform definition of it. But I think it's hard to train someone on diversity. I really feel the more exposure you get from people of different backgrounds—whether they're the same race as you or not—is really going to be what bridges the gap.

Someone on a news channel said, "Being gay is kind of like being left-handed." Back years and years ago, being left-handed was horrible and meant you were possessed by the devil. Now a lot of our young people, although not all, believe growing up that being gay isn't as big a deal. I hope that race and other differences that separate us will become like being left handed used to be.

Kareem: How do people learn from each other?

Sarah: I just got everyone's end of the year feedback and it was split. Some people really don't like forced ice breakers and other people understand it's beneficial. There's those too formal interactions, but people also get to know each other without me having to do anything. They start finding connections, and that's my favorite part of the job.

My first year, I had a GED student who was a teenage mom as a corps member and I also had a corps member who had degrees and was returning back to work after being a stay-at-home mom for her three kids. Very different people on the surface. It was interesting to watch them interact. The mom returning back to work was not only helping the teenage mom, but learning from her.

In your corps, a group of you became really tight. You went to the beach together. If you're out in a social situation—just hanging out—you start to break down barriers, trust and talk to each other. You have work as a common ground to start off the discussion. You're like, "Oh, my students are so obnoxious." Or, "They're so wonderful" and that rolls into a late night discussion where you guys solve all the world's problems.

Kareem: Can you talk about the ways that AmeriCorps tries to help its members grow?

Sarah: We have a mandate where we're supposed to provide training. As much as I thought I didn't want to be a teacher and I fought against it my whole life—

the training is my favorite part of AmeriCorps. One of the ways we try to help members grow is giving them as many opportunities as possible. Obviously, literacy-related training to help them do their jobs better, but also just being in professional experiences where they go to a national conference and learn how to behave and interact with people at those types of events. Just putting the members in a situation where they're in control—where they're the leaders.

I also think the education award—that encouragement and that bonus of saying, "You served your country, you served your community, and you deserve to do this. It's important to continue your education"—is a big step. When you're publishing your tenth book, don't be surprised when everyone comes out of the woodwork and wants to say they knew you when. Maybe, down the line, you'll move to Chicago and Miriam will be there. You can call her up and you can help each other out.

Kareem: How has the experience changed the way you see New Orleans?

Sarah: Well, I think it has to do more with the people and the programs that AmeriCorps works with. Opportunities like going to some of the Neighborhood Story Project events allow me to meet new circles of people and experience pockets of the city and culture. I grew up here and never went to a second line parade until we went to the Nine Times parade during One Book, One New Orleans. Now, I get upset when I see them and can't stop what I'm doing and start dancing. I've definitely fallen back in love with the city. However, I'm still not sure I can stay here because it's a constant love/hate relationship. Learning about how horrible the literacy

levels are, how many people want to help themselves, and how there's just not enough services is sometimes very defeating and hard to handle. You know, dealing with government agencies has just really been hard. But I have more empathy and more love of the city overall.

Kareem: Can you tell me about a time when you got your GPS stolen?

Sarah: Yeah, someone broke into the car and took the GPS, which is not a big deal. It's not like in Katrina, when we lost a third of our family photos and heirlooms. Still, it changed my perspective on the city.

I was always the kind of person that's like, "Yeah, I know the crime's bad, whatever. It's New Orleans. I grew up here. I'm gonna be okay. I'm not doing anything to bother anyone." That kind of innocence is lost now for me. I feel like I'm sacrificing a lot—giving the fact that I make little money and work a lot of hours to help people in the city—and then when you feel violated, there's definitely moments of, "Why am I doing this?" The AmeriCorps members make a lot less money. There's that constant weird guilt about saying, "You're sacrificing when my husband's in law school and I'm not paying my rent because my in-laws do." It seems like it shouldn't be a big deal. I feel stupid talking about it with you, of all people, considering you have friends and family who have had obviously much worse violence besides getting a GPS stolen.

Kareem: How has having a child changed the way you see the city?

Sarah: I see the city through very tired eyes now. I feel like Gibson's changed everything for me. I feel really lucky that I work with people who are so open to having kids at work. I always knew I wanted kids. I never really knew what I wanted career-wise. Now I look at the schools more—those types of things. I worry, "Can we afford to send him somewhere?" Owyn and I are making decisions about going to childcare. Obviously, we're looking at money because we have only have one income, but we also wanted somewhere where the people didn't all looked like him. He's one, so it's not like they're having discussions about race and background, but I think it's still really important to both of us. I guess that goes back to the segregation of the schools question earlier—finding opportunities for that is hard.

Being a mom has changed what my priorities are. I definitely work a lot less at home. My first year in AmeriCorps, I worked basically constantly. Now I get home and I'm home. Weekends I don't even turn on my computer sometimes, which is awesome, although sometimes I wish I could be sitting in front of the computer instead of chasing after Gibson and changing dirty diapers.

Kareem: What is your plan for the next few years?

Sarah: My plan for the next few months is to wait and see what happens with Owyn. I'm just waiting to see if he wants to stay here. I think I want to stay here. It depends on the day, but I feel like I'll probably stay involved in adult literacy wherever I go. I would love to do something with gardening down the line. That's when I'm happiest, besides when I'm with Gibson.

Kareem:: How has travel changed the way that you see the world?

Sarah: Travel is really important. Katrina forced people who would have never left the city to go somewhere else so they could say they don't like it and think about why they do like New Orleans. That's definitely been true for me. I mean, my parents now live in Morocco and they just bought a house in France, which is still crazy to say because they're teachers. But traveling around Morocco has given me a better understanding of different cultures. The more you can travel and the more people you can meet, you realize you're one of millions and billions of people on the earth. I hope you get to do that someday.

I think you're very open and I'm always impressed by how much you can stay above the fray despite how much has been thrown at you—many people don't. They get angry. I think it was in the last *AmeriWord* newsletter Miriam asked everyone to say a final thought and most people gave a word— "Excitement," "I'm all done"— and yours was much more deep about teaching and learning from people. You may not talk up a lot in the trainings, but I would sometimes overhear you saying something really insightful. You wait for that larger musing on the world.

Bullet holes in Kareem's car window, by Kareem Kennedy.

Senseless

The saying on the streets is: "You live by the gun, you die by the gun." I never used a gun, I was going to college, teaching school, and thought my life was on the straight and narrow path, but there was an unexpected turn.

It began late Sunday night after I got done watching the BET Awards at my cousin Brian's house in the Seventh Ward. His lady friend was over, and I wanted to give them some space, so when I got a call from a friend I knew from Delgado who needed a ride home, I was grateful for an excuse to leave the house.

It was a dark night in the Seventh Ward. When I arrived at the house, my friend had another friend with her. Her friend got into the car, and my friend said she forgot her bag and went back inside the house. When traveling late at night, I always left my car running because of what happened to Larry and other people I knew.

I sensed somebody coming out of an alley toward my side of the car. I saw an all-black silhouette, and a silver gun raise up. Everything began to happen at the same time. I saw the fire from the gun and heard

the shots. I pressed the gas pedal to the floor, and felt the third shot sting my shoulder. As I put my seat belt on, I felt that I had been shot in the stomach. The girl in the passenger seat was looking straight ahead and didn't say anything.

I moved the car as quick as I could, ignoring the stop signs and potholes—trying to get away and get to the hospital. But as I approached A.P. Tureaud, I saw flashing lights and figured that the cops could get an ambulance to me. I drove the wrong way down the street to get to the lights.

"I'm shot! I'm shot!"

The policeman asked me, "How do you know you've been shot?" That was the stupidest thing I had ever heard. My windows were shattered, and my stomach was covered with blood. The second cop told me to calm down and stay still.

Everybody was standing outside of the clubs looking at me. The ladies covered their mouths with their hands. I never lost consciousness. When the ambulance arrived, they told me to step out of the car slowly and lowered me onto the stretcher. Once I was in the ambulance, they cut my pants off.

I asked them, "Am I going to die?" and they told me, "You're going to be all right."

When I woke in the hospital bed, my body felt heavy and I was surrounded by doctors.

When I woke again, I had an IV stuck in my arm, and Brian, Steven, Kaiema, Ms. Sharon, and her daughter, Kawana, were there. She was saying a prayer over me, holding my hand. I was glad to still be alive.

When I woke again, Mario, Chevelle, April, Malika, Jason, Tiny, my mom, B-Lo and Travis were there. Next time it was Aunt Alice, Shawna, John,

Site Search   Search Local Business Listings

Search by keyword, town name, Web ID and more...

| er | Sports | Entertainment | Living | Interact | Jobs | Auto |

| litics | Education | Elections | Opinions | Business | Northshore | Vide |

EANS METRO REAL-TIME NEWS

al News from New Orleans, Louisiana

Crime Page :: Metro, Crime Page: Orleans, News, News: New Orleans »

13 shot, 3 die during violent weekend in New Orleans

By Valerie M. Faciane
June 29, 2009, 7:30PM

Police investigated two apparent murders and a handful of shootings over a violent weekend in New Orleans in which at least 13 people were shot, three of them fatally.

Reported crimes included an early-morning shooting outside Harrah's New Orleans casino, a killing in Algiers, and an incident in eastern New Orleans where seven people were sprayed with gunfire, according to New Orleans police logs released Monday morning.

According to the department's preliminary incident log, the weekend crimes kicked off with a fatal shooting at about 12:20 a.m. Saturday in Algiers.

Police found Joseph Veal on the ground in the 3300 block of Mansfield Avenu with gunshot wounds to his back and side. He died at the scene. Police have not released a possible motive or suspect in the slaying.

A few hours later, gunshots rang out outside the casino at the base of Canal Street. A 22-year-old man was waiting near South Peters Street for an acquaintance to leave the casino. He exchanged glances, and perhaps a few words, with two men who pulled up near him.

The two men opened fire on the victim, hitting him once in the thigh. The victim was taken in critical condition to a hospital and underwent surgery. Police arrested Rivers Jacques, 24, and Kyron Nelson, 22, and booked them with attempted second-degree murder. Both appeared in magistrate court Sunday and were ordered held in lieu of $500,000 bond.

Shortly before noon Saturday, a man, a woman and a 1-year-old toddler were carjacked near City Park while unloading groceries from a truck. Two gunmen approached the woman in the 4300 block of St. Ann Street and demanded she get out of the vehicle. She complied, while screaming about the baby inside the truck. The gunmen put the baby on the sidewalk and fle in the truck. No further details were released.

Four hours later, a 15-year-old boy was killed in the St. Roch neighborhood by a gunshot wound to the head, in what may have been an accidental shooting.

released any motive for the shooting.

Early Sunday, a 26-year-old man was shot in the arm in eastern New Orleans. The shooting occurred at about 4:14 a.m. in the 7800 block of Sai Street. The victim drove himself to a hospital and was listed in stable condition.

A 21-year-old man was killed Sunday night in a shooting in the 2000 block Baronne in Central City. Freddie McCoy died at the scene, according to John Gagliano, chief investigator for the coroner. McCoy was shot at about 10:1! p.m. in the arms, head and chest.

McCoy, of New Orleans, had been arrested and booked with aggravated assault and attempted murder in 2006. A jury acquitted him following a tria

About an hour after that killing, a 19-year-old man was wounded in the 18 block of Industry Street in the 7th Ward. The victim drove himself to the intersection of A.P. Tureaud Avenue and North Tonti Street. He was listed i critical condition at LSU Interim Public Hospital, according to police.

. . . .

Brendan McCarthy can be reached at bmccarthy@timespicayune.com.

Recommend (0)

Print this   **Email this**   **Share this:**

Previous story: New Orleans same-sex couple sues for marriage license

Next story: U.S. warns citizens to avoid travel to Honduras

Comments (14 total)   RSS   Post a comm

Oldest comments are shown first. Show newest comments first

Posted by savenola2
June 30, 2009, 9:48AM

And with stories like these you'd think New Orleans has a crime problem. Good thing our wise police chief is here to remind us (with statistics) that crime is actually going down. Otherwise, I'd feel really unsafe living blocks away from where people are getting mowed down as though they were fighting a war in an urban setting.

Inappropriate comment? **Alert**

Reply to this comment | **Post a new comment**

Howard, Rachel, Lindsey Miriam, and Abram.

The doctor told me the two bullets just missed my large intestine. The doctors kept telling me I was lucky, but I felt blessed.

I didn't want the Tylenol 3 they prescribed me. I wanted to smoke. My brain was still trying to swallow what had just happened and it helped me cope. Still in the hospital, I called my friend and told him to roll one up. I went downstairs and smoked it. When I got back, I didn't want the morphine because it made my groggy.

I was in the hospital for a week. I went home from the hospital to Miriam's house. She kept saying, "I can't believe this happened to you. I know you're going to get better," and took care of me until I got my strength back. She helped me bandage up the wounds every day. Seeing the actual bullet hole and the staples that went up my stomach just was a total shock.

It was difficult to move—to get in and out of cars. I felt a sharp pain in my stomach any time I coughed or made a sudden movement involving my stomach muscles. I was walking slow like an old man with a hunch in my back.

Everyone kept telling me I was smaller. It made me feel bad even though I knew they weren't saying it to hurt my feelings, just to show concern. I started going to church at St. Leo, which gave me humbleness. The stories that were written became metaphors for my recovery. The story of Paul having a thorn in his side spoke to me. I felt like the bullets were thorns of death.

The only people I really talked to were a social worker and Miriam. I would tell other people what happened, but they didn't really know how to console me.

Kareem and Miriam, by Kareem Kennedy.

A week before, I made the front page of the *The Times Picayune's* Metro section for our book with the Capdau class. Then this shit happened the next week, and I was in the Crime section of the paper for getting shot. I always read the Crime section of the newspaper and would get emotional. Like, "That ain't right." I never thought that would be me. I don't know why it happened.

I always knew Miriam was planning on moving back to Ohio to finish school after her year of AmeriCorps was over, but I kept telling myself that day would never come. She said she didn't want to go, but her rational side told her that she had to. I couldn't stop thinking that I wanted to move, too. Her last night, we hung out by the bayou, cuddling and crying together. We went back to her house and I helped her pack up to leave the next morning.

When we woke up, she told me I had to leave first so she could have a minute to herself. I walked out of the house to go to school. I turned on Bob Marley's "Could You Be Loved" and started to drive away. My phone rang. It was Miriam. I thought, "This is it! She's decided to stay." But she just wanted her i-Pod charger. It did give me a chance for one last, heartfelt kiss.

Left: Kareem was one of 13 people shot in one weekend, according to nola.com's "Crime Report."

91

Kareem with his mom, by Lea Downing.

Interview with My Mother, Marlene Kennedy

At the beginning, Miriam and I kept our relationship separate from family. I had been on my own for a few years and her people were up in Ohio. I always wanted to meet them. I don't know if she told them about me, but I talked to all my family about how much I liked her and told them, "Y'all need to accept it."

I was used to my mom being in and out of my life. After Katrina, she was staying in a trailer in Back-a-Town in the Seventh Ward. She was surrounded by drug addicts. When I would visit her, it would make me cry. She would talk about how people had messed her over, blaming everyone. I would ask her when she was going to stop.

She would just be like, "I know. I know."

During my last year of high school, I tried living with her in an apartment in the East, hoping to be that someone who helped her turn it around. Living with her was frustrating and caused us both lots of heartache. She would cook, clean, and iron my clothes, but the addiction was still there. Sometimes when I would call her out, she would talk back to me

about my own self-destructive use of weed. It was tough to hear from an addict, but that didn't make it any less true.

I moved out because it was too frustrating to watch someone I love struggle with her addiction. I needed some space because I was worried I could spiral, too. Then I started taking Mr. Gamble's class at Delgado and I started thinking I should try to understand my own family from a psychological point of view.

After I was shot, all the different parts of my world ended up in my hospital room. Miriam was there most days and my mom came as soon as she heard. I had imagined introducing them under better circumstances. I had talked about each of them to each other. My mom is hyper and full of information. When you're talking to her, you can't keep up with everything she's saying. She came into the hospital room, smiling and pacing around. She introduced herself to Miriam and asked, "You're the one who kidnapped my baby?" Miriam laughed. She inquired about her cat and talked about how thankful she was that I was okay. She decided to take a shower, and when I came out, I said, "Ma, why you taking a shower in them people's bathroom?" She said, "Boy, I had to walk a long way to get to you."

When I was finishing up this book, I started thinking about doing an interview with my mom. She's an authentically good listener, a smart reader of people, and has a good intellect. Sometimes we have such good conversations, even about her addiction, that it surprises me that she keeps doing what she's doing. Just like Miriam had done in other ways, she has shown me that love comes in all shapes and forms.

Kareem: How are you today?

Marlene: I'm a little blessed. A little blessed, not stressed as I know I'm gonna be. Glad to have you back in my world. They tell me you been busy with this book thing.

Kareem: I have been busy—very busy. What are your thoughts on me writing this book?

Marlene: I'm very proud of you. I always wanted to do an autobiography and I never got a chance to do it, and you doing it makes me feel good.

Kareem: Where did you grow up?

Marlene: I grew up in the St. Bernard housing project.

Kareem: How was it living there?

Marlene: I grew up with both parents. My dad died with cancer. He was a blueprinter for 25 years and was just about to retire. He told me, "I'm about to go home, go with the spirits."

"Going home? Where you going home at?"

I had a good father. I never heard him say a bad word a day in his life. When he died, we went to church every day but I didn't understand. I was mad with God. I rebelled against the world cause I didn't understand death. I wanted to grow up with a good husband and children because my daddy was a man and a half. I ain't met nobody like him since he passed.

My mother died in 2000. Thanksgiving morning. I was clean and sober. That was the best going home I ever saw in my life. I was at peace with death. I know

death is mandatory. I just lost a grandbaby, still going through a little emotion or grief, but I'm okay.

Kareem: Who did you grow up with?

Marlene: I grew up with the four siblings.

Kareem: Who are they?

Marlene: Jeanette, Alice, Rose, and Eddie Kennedy.

Kareem: What schools did you go to?

Marlene: I started out at John McDonogh and then I wound up going to Spectrum inside of McMain for misbehaved children.

Kareem: Can you tell me about cooking school?

Marlene: I went to Sclafani's Cooking School, completed the school, got a safety license.

Kareem: How is school different? Do you think the school has changed or do you know?

Marlene: Well, it was an upgraded school and it educated me because I was with a mixture of children with all different cultures.

Kareem: When did you first start to engage with drugs?

Marlene: I was 18. I tested marijuana—from marijuana to Valium and speed type drugs. It escalated.

Kareem: How have drugs affected your life?

Marlene: The pain has outweighed the pleasure for me. I used to enjoy it. It used to be a sociable thing for me. Now, I do it not to face some of the realities of life. I don't even feel the drugs anymore. My children are going through being rebellious against me for not being a better mother. I can't make up for the past. I can only be with them in the here and now.

Kareem: How old were you when you had your first child?

Marlene: I was 20.

Kareem: When when did you realize that you couldn't handle the responsibility of raising children?

Marlene: Well, when my life got unmanageable, I rather seen y'all in a safe environment than with me with my addiction. My addiction was overwhelming. Then my family started fighting with the state, trying to take you all. You know, I gave you to them.

Kareem: Were you worried about the safety of your children?

Marlene: Of course I was. Of course I was. I would die for my children—put anything down and walk an extra mile for them.

Kareem: How many children do you have?

Marlene: I have nine living children, and I had one abortion and one miscarriage.

Kareem: Do you have a favorite?

Marlene: I don't have a favorite child. The child that's going through life difficulties will be the favorite—that's the one that really has a need.

Kareem: Do you feel rejected by your children?

Marlene: Yes I do, yes I do, yes I do, yes I do, yes I do.

Kareem: In what ways?

Marlene: Because of the disrespect and the rebelliousness. They don't love me in my addiction. They're supposed to not enable me, but just love me until I'm able to love myself. Don't judge me as a person because I'm a mother and a half and I accept them in their shortcomings. But they can disrespect me, curse me out, spit in my face. I had it all done to me, but I still love my children. I might not love myself, but I do love my children.

Kareem: Do you feel outcast by family because of your drug usage?

Marlene: Yes, yes, yes.

Kareem: Can you tell me a story of when you felt guilty for not being there?

Marlene: I felt guilty about not being supportive enough for different occasions. I felt guilty about not being there for your graduation.

Kareem: Why did you decide to name me Kareem?

Marlene: Because I felt like it was a strong name. You know, your father was into Allah and then the basketball player. I felt like he was a strong guy and you were a strong boy—a good, loving boy. You support me. I miss you so much. You're not sharing enough time with me.

Kareem: Can you tell me about my father?

Marlene: Your daddy was a good father but a controlling father. He used religious belief to manipulate, and my mother opened my eyes. She was an older, wiser woman. He was a Muslim and he was a big worshipper when it came to religion.

Kareem: How did you meet?

Marlene: I met him in the St. Bernard Project. His name is Douglas Jones. You don't mind if I smoke a cigarette?

Kareem: Why do you think my siblings' fathers and my father didn't do their jobs?

Marlene: My mother played a great part of that, too. She didn't want to cut me aloose, let me go. After my dad died, she wanted to hold control. She felt like I didn't need a man. "Mama taking care of you, you don't need that daddy." My mother had a lot of control and I lived with my mother.

Kareem: Why do you think your drug use has lasted so long?

Marlene: Because I haven't totally surrendered. I keep on looking back instead of just letting go. That's one of the reasons. I've been to recovery programs and psychiatrists, but I feel like if I totally surrender to God and give my total time to him, He will take it away. I haven't had the strong desire to cut it, let it go.

Right now, I'm not being around positive people. It's a materialistic world where everybody's having a hard time, but not respecting my pain and my needs. You know, a walk in the park or just conversations. I be so excited when I see you because you lay on that sofa and I lay on this sofa and we'd chitchat and laugh.

Kareem: Why did you go to jail and what was it like?

Marlene: I got arrested for shoplifting. I've never done longer than 16 months, but I did 22 years of my life back and forth.

Kareem: What was it like in jail?

Marlene: I found serenity and got my spirituality up. I didn't entertain the foolishness, the madness going on. I was content and off into my own world. They say be contented in any circumstances. Peter and Paul went to jail and God opened doors for them. He's always been there for me. Even when men say one thing, I always trust in God for my freedom.

Kareem: What do you see yourself doing in the next five years?

Marlene: Relaxing and waiting to feed y'all or hoping y'all come with your new wives, lives, and whatever. I'll be laid-back, relaxed, retired. Right now I'm unemployed. I'm mentally incompetent due to the Katrina storm. I have flashbacks.

Kareem: What is one of your proudest moments?

Marlene: One of my proudest moments? To see y'all do completion in school. Y'all's education. And your graduating last year.

Kareem: Can you share some of the words you hear?

Marlene: I need to say don't judge a person. Pray for that person to change and better themselves. Addiction is like sin. Sin is sin in the eyes of God— whether I have sex without marriage or kill or steal—sin is still sin in the eyes of God. God'll use me as a vessel to clean me up one day so I can tell somebody where I've been and where I come from. But who am I to judge you? Obama, Michael Jackson. Whether I have money, or am broke, I'm still somebody. I thank God everyday for waking up because somebody didn't wake up. All those Christians that say they're a Christian and say hallelujah, praise God and turn they back and shun other people, they not are real people.

It's about saving souls, winning souls, encouraging one another. That's what life is about and that's all. That's all I can say. If I can't help you, I'm not gonna hurt you. If I can't tell you something positive, I'm not gonna bring you down. Who am I to judge? And one day, God will deliver me. You'll see the God in me—no psychiatrist, no person badgering me or nothing else. I won't die in my sin. He got something in store for me. I tried suicide and all that, homicide and all that. Even though I'm living in my sinful nature, I still trust God, some supreme being.

Kareem: When I got shot, what were your thoughts?

Marlene: Oh man, my thoughts was, "Oh God, please don't take one of my children away from me." I was devastated because you were here that Sunday with me and this girl kept callin' for you to come away. You had just went to church, came, and spent the day. The more hurting part about it, I didn't find out about it until the next day. I thank God. That's my scariest thing in life, man—taking one of my children. The devil'll use that to tear me up more. I'd rather go first.

Kareem: What was your impression of Miriam?

Marlene: Oh, great, beautiful person, beautiful, down to earth. I thought she was go be my daughter-in-law. I thought she was. I wanted her to be.

Kareem: If you could change one thing in your life what would it be?

Marlene: For all my family to be on one accord, unity, togetherness. That'll make me the happiest person in the world for us to sit around the table, laugh, talk, chat, and be as one.

Kareem: How is your relationship now with your children?

Marlene: It's trying to get better. I just have to allow them to be where they're at. I don't want to see them hurt. I've been there already. So that's why I'm getting your birthday party together so we can all come together as one. That's what it's mainly about.

Kareem and Marlene at his birthday party, October 31, 2009, by Rachel Breunlin.

NSP AFTERWORD

December 2009

It has been a long four years for the Neighborhood Story Project since the last series of books by John McDonogh students came out. In June of 2005, we were riding high, with five books by high school students circulating the city and neighborhoods were they were written. After Harry Potter, they were the best sellers in the city.

And in August of 2005 we were back at John McDonogh, with 60 applicants for the next round of book-making, and went home for a weekend of sorting applications. On Monday, the levees failed, and the applications were waiting on Rachel's kitchen table when we got back to town seven weeks later, a grim reminder of one more thing lost.

The NSP set about the work it knew, making books with Nine Times Social and Pleasure Club, making posters about the Seventh Ward, and a book of community gathering spots—Cornerstones. But through it all we wanted to go back to John McDonogh and hear what was happening in teenage-land.

So in the fall of 2007, we went recruiting at John Mac. We were holding the first round of books, relics of the pre-storm era, and very few of the new students had heard of them. There were five brave souls who signed up for a class in book-making. Daron Crawford, Susan Henry, Kareem Kennedy, Kenneth Phillips, and Pernell Russell.

The first part was the easiest. We read the first round of NSP books and the classics like: *Life and Death on the South Side of Chicago*, and Sherman Alexie's *Lone Ranger and Tonto Firstfight in Heaven*.

And then we started on the two and a half year journey of writing our stories. We wrote about life before Katrina, and some of the Katrina experience, but we mostly worked on Documenting the Now.

The Now was ever-changing: Daron moved from house to house, and studio to studio. Kareem went from high school student to Delgado student. Pernell went from nearly carefree (dancing, making clothes) to dealing with loss. Susan's career in fashion and cosmetology went from theoretical to real. Kenneth worked on his anger management, while getting learning about his past.

We began to talk about the need to have something at stake in the book—the need to represent our struggles and not just the things that we wanted people to know about our lives. Or as Kareem Kennedy put it to everyone, "People want to read your mind to ease their mind."

And so we started in on the writing the hard parts. We went to where the projects were in the process of being torn down. Sneaking in through holes in fences, we roamed where the thousands lived, now desolate and post-apocalyptic. We went to the new spaces, shotgun doubles, ranch homes in the suburbs, and we wrote to make sense of the changes.

Rachel taught interviewing and ethnography—how to de-familiarize yourself with your surroundings and connect your personal stories to the larger cultures of New Orleans. Abram taught writing styles. Lea and Lindsey went with the writers to interview and photograph.

During 2008 we kept at it, interviewing family, former neighbors, other people who could help broaden their perspectives on themes in the books.

In March of 2008 the NSP published *The House of Dance and Feathers: A Museum by Ronald Lewis*, and the writers got to see their first NSP book release party-in Ronald's backyard in the Lower Ninth Ward, Mardi Gras Indians and Brass Bands. Two hundred people dancing in the rain.

As Rachel turned her attention from editing *The House of Dance and Feathers* toward working on building up the structures of the four books, the work kicked into overdrive. Weekends became an abstract idea, as writers and NSP staff started to live in our office in Seventh Ward. We took occasional breaks to go back out and get more photos, or to get the interviewees more involved in the editing process.

In September of 2009 we printed out what we had and gave copies to family and friends and impartial readers. They came together as book committees, telling us what they liked and what the books needed to feel finished. We took notes, gave ourselves a weekend off, and then got back on the horse.

October was the end of the road. We had to weigh what pieces stayed in, how to tell the untold parts. Hard decisions as the idea of the books met the reality of paper and print. Late nights and early mornings led to this—four new books, five new authors, and a return to the roots of the NSP.

NSP'S HUGE LIST OF THANK-YOUS

Our first and biggest thank-you to our authors and their families: Daron Crawford, Susan Henry, Kareem Kennedy, Kenneth Phillips, and Pernell Russell. It has been two great years of getting to know y'all, and a huge honor to be so involved in your lives. We are proud of your work, and feel blessed to have become family. We look forward to knowing y'all and reading y'all for years to come.

To the mighty University of New Orleans—the College of Liberal Arts, the College of Education, and UNO Press: We are grateful and proud to be a part of the University community. Thank you to Chancellor Ryan, Susan Krantz, Rick Barton, Bob Cashner, Joe King, and Anthony Cipolone. In Anthropology, thank you to David Beriss, Jeffrey Ehrenreich, and Martha Ward. In the College of Education, thank you to Jim Meza, Andre Perry, and April Whatley Bedford. At UNO Press, Bill Lavender and GK Darby.

To all the people who have supported the NSP, thank you. Huge gratitude to all of the writers at the write-a-thon, without whom we could not have made this milestone. We look forward to out-writing last year's amazingness.

To the Lupin Foundation. Thank you for your consistent support over the years. These books could not have happened without you.

To our John McDonogh Senior High/ RSD family—Principal Gerald Debose, Antoinette Pratcher, Dawn Greay, Alicia Carter Watts, Shawon Bernard, Brother Jamal Robertson, Deborah Richardson, Nira Cooper and all of the other teachers at the Mac. Thank you for working with us and for being so supportive of the efforts of the NSP.

Thank you to the Cowan Family and Jewish Funds for Justice. Your gift kept us going, and Paul's legacy continues to inspire us.

To Gareth, thank you for going above and beyond, once again, to balance a crazy amount of work with beautiful design.

For getting us ready to go to press, Felicia McCarren, Jordan Flaherty, Siobhan Flahive McKieran, Ariella Cohen, GK Darby, Bill Lavender, Hot Iron Press, and Eve Abrams.

To the Bard Early College in New Orleans program and Stephen Tremaine: thank you for being an awesome partner in this work.

To our board—Petrice Sams Abiodun, Susan Krantz, Corlita Mahr Spreen, Troy Materre, Helen Regis, and Emelda Wylie. It has been a great journey with y'all, and we are looking forward to more.

Thank you to the Zeitoun Foundation for supporting the work. Your unsolicited gift was a huge boost to our organization, and your story of reclaiming against great odds has been part of our inspiration.

And to our families: Dan and Max Omar Etheridge; Cynthia Breunlin, Doug Breunlin and Nanci Gordon, Megan Etheridge, and Kate, Tommaso, and Zoe Weichmann (for stepping in to help take care of Rachel's men while she was on editing lockdown); Nolan Marshall, Tessa Corthell, Shana Sassoon, Phyllis, Linda and Jerry, the Hsiangs, the Downings, the Darnells: thank you for being our family through this process. We could not have done it without you, and we are glad we didn't have to try.

Viva New Orleans

Rachel Breunlin, Lindsey Darnell, Lea Downing and Abram Himelstein

Neighborhood Story Project

Postscript

Notes on the release of the Third Edition

It has been five years since we released *Aunt Alice vs Bob Marley*. In those five years, the book has developed a mind of its own, going into the hearts of people and places far beyond the confines of the NSP's writing lab.

When I think about how the book lives, I sometimes think about how human boundaries and social constructs impede interesting interaction, and I am happy, because I think the book carefully carves out that unique life—creating a conversation where it would not exist. *Aunt Alice vs Bob Marley* was always intended to keep it real. I wanted the book to pay homage to the people and places that make New Orleans special. The ones on the bumpy back blocks: the children, the women, and the men who are the fabric that holds culture and communities together.

Five years is a long time for a twenty-five year old. Since the 2010 release I have graduated from Southern University at New Orleans with a bachelors of Social Work degree, and have held my first full-time job, as Client Advocate for the Orleans Parish Public Defender's office.

And during these five years, the losses of my loved ones have continued to mount. Since publishing in 2010, my Aunt Rose, my cousin Bryan Washington, and my friends Rayel Adams, Ashley Blunt, and Michael Broyard have passed on. And on August 26, 2014, my sister Kaiema "Kema" Kennedy was killed while sitting peacefully on her front porch, six days after her 26th birthday. Kema's birthday cake sat on the table waiting for me or one of her loved ones to finish it off.

Of all of the many deaths, this one hit me the hardest. Kema and I had a strong brother-sister relationship that was rooted in love for family. Every family tree has many branches. Kema was the sweetest fruit on our family tree and would treat a beggar on the street with the same respect she'd give an elder in the community. Kema had the brightest smile, capable of lighting any dim space. I remember when I was shot the look of hurt and worry on her face as I lay in the hospital bed. Now I have the same hurt and worry that she felt for me, permanently, in my heart. I am trying to turn this pain from Kema's passing into strength to carry on.

Kema wanted to travel and explore the world. After she read my book, she told me she wanted to write one of her own, but make hers more juicy. She wanted to have her family be of one accord, under love. I hope to carry on Kema's name for as long as I live and take with me the good things she imparted. My hope is that one day we will never have to mourn a loved one's death due to violence. We have to stop the killing and start the living. Long live Kema! Long live Kema! Long live Kema!

♥ 19 likes

kai2201 Brother you know you my heartbeat 365
this love we share is amazing HAPPPPPPPY BORN
DAY BABBBBYYYY 🗣️🧠🎂👄💥💦🎉🎊